Praise for *Hope for Your Marriage*

"Clayton and Ashlee Hurst are on the forefront of marriage ministry. This book is full of practical wisdom that's a must-read for anyone looking to grow in their marriage."

—Jimmy Evans, founder and CEO,
MarriageToday, Southlake, Texas

"This book, layered with scriptures and personal stories of overcoming obstacles, will bless every couple ready to have a healthy and happy marriage with God at the center!"

—DeVon Franklin, CEO, Franklin Entertainment;
bestselling author of *The Hollywood
Commandments*, *The Wait*, and *Produced by Faith*

"Whether you are a newlywed or married for decades, this encouraging book will give you new and practical insight into how to make your marriage the best relationship in your life."

—Shaunti Feldhahn, social researcher; bestselling
author of *For Women Only*, *For Men Only*, and *The
Surprising Secrets of Highly Happy Marriages*

"We encourage every married couple to not just buy this book, but live with it, mine its depths, and live out its principles. You will be better for it!"

—John and Aventer Gray, Associate Pastor of Lakewood
Church; Director of Dance at Lakewood Church

"Ashlee and Clayton transparently tell their story of honestly misunderstanding each other—a story of every husband and wife! Yet, God revealed insights that enabled them to love and respect each other in meaningful and friendly ways. We are blessed by their lives and testimony."

—Dr. Emerson and Sarah Eggerichs, Love and Respect Ministries

"Written out of the overflow of their own journey, Clayton and Ashlee share how God transformed their marriage. A hope-filled book for all those who desire a loving, supportive relationship."

—Gary Chapman, Ph.D., bestselling author
of *The Five Love Languages*

"With practical wisdom and real-life application, Clayton and Ashlee provide a treasure-trove of insights for building a God-honoring marriage. Every couple needs to read this fantastic book!"

—Drs. Les and Leslie Parrott, #1 *New York Times* bestselling
authors of *Saving Your Marriage Before It Starts*

"Read this book. Not only will it help you increase marital satisfaction, but it will lead toward a marriage you never dreamed possible."

—Ted Cunningham, pastor, Woodland Hills Family Church,
Branson, Missouri; author of *Fun Loving You*

"The key to success in any media, especially as authors, is to identify so thoroughly with the audience that they feel the story is about themselves. That's what Clayton and Ashlee Hurst have so masterfully achieved. If you want a great marriage, not just a good one, read this book!"

—SQuire Rushnell and Louise DuArt, *New York
Times* bestselling authors of Godwinks book
series and *The 40 Day Prayer Challenge*

"You're holding the quintessential playbook for a thriving marriage. No matter what marital season you find yourself in, this incredible resource will help you take your most-prized earthly relationship to the next level."

—Chris Brown, pastor, speaker, Ramsey Personality,
nationally syndicated radio host of *Life Money Hope*

"Read it. Your marriage will be glad you did!"

—Ted Lowe, author of *Your Best Us* and founder of marriedpeople.org

HOPE
FOR YOUR
MARRIAGE

EXPERIENCE GOD'S GREATEST DESIRES
FOR YOU AND YOUR SPOUSE

clayton & ashlee hurst

EMANATE
BOOKS

Published in Nashville, Tennessee, by Emanate Books, an imprint of Thomas Nelson. Emanate Books and Thomas Nelson are registered trademarks of HarperCollins Christian Publishing, Inc.

Thomas Nelson titles may be purchased in bulk for educational, business, fund-raising, or sales promotional use. For information, please e-mail SpecialMarkets@ThomasNelson.com.

Unless otherwise noted, Scripture quotations are from the Holy Bible, New International Version®, NIV®. Copyright © 1973, 1978, 1984, 2011 by Biblica, Inc.® Used by permission of Zondervan. All rights reserved worldwide. www.Zondervan.com. The "NIV" and "New International Version" are trademarks registered in the United States Patent and Trademark Office by Biblica, Inc.®

Scripture quotations marked ESV are from the ESV® Bible (The Holy Bible, English Standard Version®). Copyright © 2001 by Crossway, a publishing ministry of Good News Publishers. Used by permission. All rights reserved.

Scripture quotations marked NLT are from the Holy Bible, New Living Translation. © 1996, 2004, 2007, 2013, 2015 by Tyndale House Foundation. Used by permission of Tyndale House Publishers, Inc., Carol Stream, Illinois 60188. All rights reserved.

Scripture quotations marked TLB are from The Living Bible. Copyright © 1971. Used by permission of Tyndale House Publishers, Inc., Carol Stream, Illinois 60188. All rights reserved.

Scripture quotations marked KJV are from the King James Version. Public domain.

Scripture quotations marked THE MESSAGE are from *The Message*. Copyright © by Eugene H. Peterson 1993, 1994, 1995, 1996, 2000, 2001, 2002. Used by permission of NavPress. All rights reserved. Represented by Tyndale House Publishers, Inc.

Scripture quotations marked NKJV are from the New King James Version®. © 1982 by Thomas Nelson. Used by permission. All rights reserved.

Any Internet addresses, phone numbers, or company or product information printed in this book are offered as a resource and are not intended in any way to be or to imply an endorsement by Thomas Nelson, nor does Thomas Nelson vouch for the existence, content, or services of these sites, phone numbers, companies, or products beyond the life of this book.

ISBN 978-0-7852-1638-4 (eBook)
ISBN 978-0-7852-1645-2 (TP)

Library of Congress Control Number: 2017956694

Printed in the United States of America
18 19 20 21 22 LSC 10 9 8 7 6 5 4 3 2 1

*We pray many marriages will find the
hope they need within these pages.
Even the marriages yet to be created.*

Let this be written for a future generation,
that a people not yet created may praise the LORD.

—PSALM 102:18

Contents

Foreword

Years ago, my father was frustrated with my mother and decided to give her the silent treatment. Or, as we call it, the "cold shoulder-deluxe." He went around all day not speaking to her, and when he had to speak he would only give a one word answer. Well, this went on for a few hours until my mother had had enough. She went and quietly hid herself behind a door without telling anyone. She remained as still and quiet as she could, until finally my father got worried because he hadn't seen her in a while. He began searching the house. He looked, and looked. Then, when he walked right by, she jumped out on his back, scaring him and saying, "I am not getting off until you cheer up!" They laughed and laughed until my father could no longer remember what he was upset about.

Every couple will face difficulty in marriage, but the ones who learn how to overcome disagreements are the ones who will succeed.

Today, some of the greatest spiritual attacks are on our homes. The enemy works hard to divide families and bring strife into marriages. That's why it is so vital for us to learn how to fight for our most important relationships.

Clayton and Ashlee Hurst have served faithfully here at Lakewood Church for more than a decade. We love the joy and leadership they bring to our family of ministries. Victoria and I have appreciated both their commitment to each other and their commitment to the people of Lakewood, and that's why we asked them to oversee the marriage and parenting ministry here at Lakewood.

Clayton and Ashlee will be the first to tell you they are not perfect. They don't have all the answers. But what they do have is a willingness to share all the ways God has worked in their marriage over the years knowing that if He did it for them, He will do it for you too.

In *Hope for Your Marriage*, Clayton and Ashlee openly share the difficulty they faced in their first five years of marriage. Young married couples often don't realize what is going wrong and Clayton and Ashlee were no different. They didn't know what they didn't know. Slowly, over time, as they let God work in their relationship, they began to see the fruit.

In *Hope for Your Marriage* you will find encouragement for your marriage no matter where you are on your journey. Maybe you're engaged and wondering what the days ahead hold for you. This book is for you. Maybe you are a newly-wed, enjoying the afterglow of your honeymoon. This book is for you. Maybe you've made it through the first twenty years of marriage and are searching for a fresh wind in your relationship. This book is for you too. Or maybe you've been through a lot of pain in your marriage and are considering a separation. Yes, *Hope for Your Marriage* is for you too.

No matter where you are in your marriage, stay committed to your spouse and watch what God does on your behalf. Remain faithful and don't quit. Your family and friends will see the difference. God will also see the difference and honor you for it.

There is hope for your marriage!

Pastor Joel Osteen
Lakewood Church

1

Dry Bones Come Alive

"Son of man, can these bones live?"

—Ezekiel 37:3

They say a person needs just three things to
be truly happy in this world: someone to love,
something to do, and something to hope for.

—Tom Bodett, author and radio host

*Are you willing to do whatever it takes to have the marriage
you always dreamed of?*

At the very beginning of our marriage, we would have
answered that question with a resounding *yes*! And if someone had challenged us with that question during the early
years of our marriage, it could have changed the trajectory
of our marriage.

On June 15, 1996, our wedding day, we began what we thought would be our uninterrupted, lifelong love affair. We were in love and all our energy had been spent planning and preparing for our big day. We picked out color schemes, decided whether to use real or fake flowers, and talked about whether eight attendants each were too many. The small details were important to us. We were both very proud of our Christian heritage and wanted everyone to know that our wedding day was dedicated to God and to the beginning of our commitment to each other. We had been engaged for about eight months, and the time had flown by quickly. Before we knew it, the pictures had been taken, the reception was over, and we were off on a romantic honeymoon. We were finally married, on top of the world, and nothing would ever change that—right?

In retrospect, we spent so much time preparing for our wedding day that we didn't prepare much for the days that would follow. In our premarital counseling sessions, we were assured that since our parents had great marriages, we should be fine and there was no need to discuss anything deep concerning our relationship. And we believed it. We had a false sense of security. We thought there was no need to continue premarital counseling.

During that first year, we were redefining what normal looked like. We were learning how to be married, how to be a husband and a wife, and how to love each other on a new level. Honestly, we began that year on a mountaintop and then began our slow descent. We had no idea we were heading directly into a valley. A deep and painful valley. Almost five years later we found ourselves stuck in that valley. We had done so many hurtful things to each other we didn't know if there was any way out.

There is a story in the Bible that describes a similar desolate valley. The prophet Ezekiel was swept away into a panoramic vision by God. The Lord placed him in the middle of a valley full of dry bones. Suddenly, God took him up in the air to survey the scene of destruction. As far as Ezekiel could see in any direction was nothing but death and despair. A broad valley filled with dried bones, scattered from east to west. It was the valley of death and all hope was gone. Or was it?

Our Valley Moment

Our valley moment came early on in our marriage when we realized we did not know how to effectively communicate with each other. Often we found ourselves yelling back and forth, trying to get our points across. We were miserable. We thought we had tried everything but nothing seemed to work. At that moment, we were desperate for hope! We were faced with the same questions we now ask other couples:

Were we willing to do whatever it took to have the marriage we had always hoped and dreamed of?

Were we willing to take small steps every day to get out of this hopeless valley we found ourselves in?

Were we willing to submit to God and to each other?

From Ashlee

It was November 2000. During the presidential election, as the world was debating and arguing over hanging chads, I was debating over a marriage hanging on by a thread. I had given birth to our first child just five weeks earlier. And as the world was thrust into chaos, I felt a chaos of uncertainty in my own heart of what the upcoming years had in store. *How could we bring a new addition into our little family when our marriage felt lifeless? Why were we so unhappy? Why didn't we have a successful marriage? Both sets of our parents had been successful, both of us were raised in Christian homes, and we were very involved in our church.* I started thinking back over the last five years and what had gone wrong. I started picturing it in bullet points.

- Year 1: The first few months were exciting and fun, almost like living Christmas day over and over. We lived in the cutest little log cabin in a hayfield with cows all around us. It was any country girl's dream. It was our own little East Texas paradise. We were happy. Clayton did have a few quirks that I thought were a little strange, but I was convinced I could eventually change him. I did, however, have some silent internal struggles from my past that I never shared with Clayton, but for the most part it was like dating, only we never had to say goodnight and leave.
- Year 2: The honeymoon phase was ending. When we tried to talk to each other, we would find ourselves

disagreeing on almost everything. Those disagreements turned into hurtful arguments. I had just started my first year teaching high school and I was not enjoying it. I was young to be teaching high school students and felt overwhelmed. I tried to talk to Clayton about it so he could encourage me through it, but he just tried to fix all my problems. I didn't want that, I just wanted him to listen. I stopped sharing as much as I used to with him.

- Year 3: Clayton took a position as the children's pastor at our church. I was now a "pastor's wife." I was twenty-three years old and felt very unqualified. *I don't know how to play the piano, preach, or sing,* I thought. *How am I going to be a preacher's wife?* I had ideas of what kind of woman I now needed to be and in my mind, I was a big failure, but I could never share this with Clayton. He would just try to fix it. I began to slowly close myself off from him, and I started dying inside.

- Year 4: I hated sex. Those silent struggles from my past were starting to creep in on me in ways that I could no longer bury. A well-meaning person I confided my struggles to, however, told me I just needed to endure the fifteen minutes and I would be fulfilling my husband and that it was my duty as a wife to do so.

- Year 5: Everything was just too much—the terrible communication, the unfulfilled sex life, the idea that we needed to have this perfect marriage, and now a baby. I couldn't take it anymore. I felt trapped in a broken relationship, I felt trapped in an identity of unworthiness, I felt trapped in this new role as a mom, and I was depressed. I had thoughts of ending my life because I saw no other way out. I was in the valley of dry bones and I was dying.

From Clayton

I remember that fifth year being a pivotal time for us. We were struggling more than ever in our relationship. I remember being so overwhelmed by guilt, condemnation, and sadness. We were supposed to make it. In fact, not just make it, we should have been the poster couple for a perfect marriage. Our parents' marriages were successful and everyone assumed we would follow in their footsteps. We had a lot going for us, but our marriage was in a downward spiral with no hope in sight.

I had never felt so much pressure to keep it all together. There was such weight to be perfect and we were nowhere close. In fact, no one knew just how badly we were struggling. There was no way anyone could have known because we had become experts at putting on masks to cover our pain. People in our church were looking to us to lead the way. I felt that I was failing as a pastor and as a husband. Now with a baby on the way, I was destined to continue to fail.

Many times I felt as though I was swimming in the middle of the ocean and heading in one direction for what seemed like an eternity only to realize there was no land in sight. Then I would try something else and "swim" in the opposite direction and still see no land. I felt as if I was overwhelmed and about to drown. It was such a frustrating time. Our marriage wasn't supposed to fail. How had we fallen into such a place of desperation? Here are my thoughts looking back over those first five years.

- Year 1: We had nothing but each other in the beginning. I was working at the university where Ashlee was finishing her degree. We lived out in the middle of a hayfield in a log cabin that belonged to my family. It was a simple life, and we were trying to establish a new normal for us both. It was exciting, and we were in love.
- Year 2: The honeymoon was over. Ashlee had begun her first year of teaching. She was frustrated day after day. She would come home and tell me all her problems and I felt as if she wanted me to be her savior. I remember one day when she began telling me her problems, and I had all I could stand. Obviously, she needed my help, so I began instructing her on how to fix things. Yelling, she said, "Would you quit trying to fix my problems and just listen?" I thought that was probably the stupidest thing I had ever heard. I was so frustrated that she wouldn't let me help. I was failing as a husband, but at work I was excelling. The university I worked for began investing in me and sending me out of state for training sessions. My bosses seemed to be pleased with everything I was doing. Finally, I was being appreciated!

- Year 3: I continued advancing at work but I was ready for a change. I had been faithful to serve in our local church, and each Wednesday night I rushed home from work and then headed out to teach elementary kids at church. This provided another way to receive the love and appreciation that I wasn't getting from Ashlee. Midway through this year I was offered the position of children's pastor at our church. For a man, there is nothing quite like the feeling of being wanted or needed. The church wanted me to become a full-time pastor, which I had known I was supposed to do for a long time, but Ashlee was hesitant and scared. She told me she didn't want me to take the job, but I took it anyway.

- Year 4: Our relationship was continuing to sink deeper and deeper into despair. I was numb. I didn't seem to care. We bought our first house, so I felt more like a provider, however dysfunctional I was. My fulfillment was coming from helping others at the church. People around us thought everything was great because we were experts at wearing masks and speaking the right language. All the while, we were dying inside and our hope for a great marriage was fading fast.

- Year 5: Ashlee and I were nothing but roommates. We wore our wedding rings but, honestly, we were simply coexisting under the same roof. My work was continuing to thrive, and I was finding my passion and voice through it. Then things intensified after Ashlee gave birth to our first child. How in the world could I be a good father when I couldn't even be a good husband? What should have been some of the happiest times in our marriage were turning into a valley of death.

We wish another couple had set us down and told us their story—their challenges and their triumphs. It would have helped us know that there was hope no matter how bad things seemed. If we had understood that God was fighting for us and that He didn't bring us together to fail, it would have helped us a lot. We wish we had been more open about our relationship and had realized that every married couple faces challenges. Back then we didn't know that marriage isn't just about making each other happy; it's also about making us holy. God uses our spouses to reveal the areas that need the most attention in our lives. If only we had laid our pride down and decided to love each other, oh what a difference that would have made!

Hope for our marriage was always there; we just didn't realize how to tap into it.

We have talked with many couples who found themselves in a valley just like ours. And as with us, it didn't happen overnight. They had been descending into the valley for some time when they suddenly realized they had lost all hope. It's almost as if they had been slowly dying.

Many times, couples become complacent with where they are and slowly their relationship begins to die. We tell these couples to recognize where they are in the valley and decide to make a change. Usually the change isn't earth shattering. Most of the time it's something small, but a small change can have an incredible impact. Just like a spark that can become a roaring fire. We often instruct couples to simply begin changing how they respond to situations. Where once they were negative, now they recognized an opportunity to respond in a more positive and encouraging way.

This is exactly what happened to the first couple I ever gave marital advice to. Ashlee and I had the opportunity to share our testimony for the first time at a marriage event at our home church right before we moved to Houston. We were excited and anxious to share some of the struggles we had encountered during those first five years. About a week after the event, I received a phone call from someone who had attended and wanted some marital advice. I was shocked by the phone call and immediately began to pray for guidance because the person on the other end of that call was my mom.

My mom and dad had been in the audience the night we spoke. They had been married more than forty years and most people, including myself, would have assumed that their marriage was as strong as ever. My mom and dad, however, were facing new challenges and needed to learn how to communicate all over again. This was a shock to me because I had never seen them upset with each other or even argue very much.

We were a normal family in a small East Texas town. My dad (Bill) worked for a local bank and my mom (Judy) was a kindergarten teacher. They seemed to have a good marriage. I remember my dad coming home from work and always kissing my mom while she was working in the kitchen. We went to church almost every time the doors were open. I was certain my parents had the perfect relationship because of what I saw growing up. They seemed to have it all figured out. On the surface, everything was fine.

My parents had successfully raised three great kids, and as they were in the middle of their empty-nest stage of life, they realized they were in a valley. They weren't sure how they got there but wanted to get out and fast. Dad and Mom decided to swallow their pride and get to work. They found a local Christian counselor who helped them in their journey to get out of their valley of dry bones. Although they had been married for many years, they realized they needed help. They chose to make some small adjustments in how they responded and reacted to each other. They began to establish some new habits that would impact their relationship for years to come. As I write, they have been married well over fifty years and are helping other married couples get out of the valley.

Can you imagine what was going through Ezekiel's mind as he saw the bones? Surely he wasn't thinking that God was going to challenge him. God asked him an impossible question and then something extraordinary happened. Ezekiel saw God perform a miracle but it happened because he focused on God and not on the circumstances around him.

Even though there was nothing but dried, sun-bleached bones around him, Ezekiel's response was filled with hope. "Only You know!" he said. In other words, Ezekiel wasn't moved by what he saw or even by how he felt. Ezekiel was moved by the hand that held the world in place. His response was not a closing statement but an opening declaration! The Bible says that "faith pleases God." It doesn't talk about the *amount* of faith that pleases Him. It's a good thing God doesn't require large amounts of faith to cause Him to respond. He is the God of hope. He is the God of restoration. He is the God of the impossible and nothing is too difficult for Him.

Your Part

Ezekiel had his part to play. Ezekiel had to take God at His word and begin to declare life out loud over a dead situation. God was helping Ezekiel begin to understand the power of the spoken word. God could have just raised the dead bones back to life, but He decided to teach Ezekiel a lesson that would one day help us all. If we go back to Genesis, you can see that He could have just thought about light and the light would have come. Instead, God declared, "Let there be light!" and there was light. God set the standard of declaring hope and life at the very beginning.

In marriage, we each have our part to play. Regardless of how good or bad it may feel right now, you have the choice to make it better. Ezekiel had to *speak* to the bones. For God to do a miracle in your relationship, you must begin by believing God and declaring life over your dead situation. A great thing to do is to declare what God's Word says about marriage in general. You could say something like, "God, You said in Ecclesiastes 4 that a threefold cord is not quickly broken. Thank You that regardless of how I feel today, our covenant won't be broken."

Simply begin thanking God for your spouse. "He who finds a wife finds a good thing, and obtains favor from the LORD" (Prov. 18:22 NKJV). Having a grateful heart seems to always change the temperature around you. You are choosing to be a thermostat instead of a thermometer. Don't just describe how you feel or what you see. Declare over your marriage what it will become.

As we began our fifth year we had to decide, as Ezekiel did, to focus on God and not on the circumstances around us. Like Ezekiel, we didn't use our words to describe how bad our marriage was, we used our words to declare that with God we can do all things! We didn't see a transformation overnight, but we began to make small changes in how we communicated. We started honestly sharing how we were feeling and gave each other the space to make mistakes along the way.

Clayton: I remember during this time a couple who came to me for help. The wife approached me one day and asked if I would counsel her and her husband. I told her I would, even though I needed counseling myself. We met every week for about a month and I thought we were making good progress. It turned out, however, that at the end of our time together they were worse than when we began. I remember getting very frustrated with this couple. *Why weren't they willing to make the changes they needed to save their marriage?* I wondered.

I was blind to the irony. I was telling them how to fix their marriage, when I didn't have the slightest clue how to fix my own.

After this miserable experience, I made a promise to myself: I would never counsel another couple without first asking them, "Are you willing to do whatever it takes to have the marriage that you have always hoped and dreamed of?"

If a couple says yes, then we proceed, but if they aren't sure, then I delay counseling until their answer is a clear yes. After promising myself to approach counseling couples in this way, I sensed God asking me a question. It wasn't an audible voice but something He impressed on my heart: "Clayton, are you willing to do whatever it takes to have the marriage that you have always hoped and dreamed of?"

Me? I thought. *What about Ashlee? I try to talk to her and she shuts me out.*

Again, God asked, "Clayton, are you willing to do whatever it takes to have the marriage that you have always hoped and dreamed of?"

"Yes, God," I said.

As I began to humble myself, God began to soften my heart.

Small Steps

When we were in the middle of the valley, completely over-whelmed by hopelessness, the goodness and grace of God was our guiding light. We had three options: continue to live as we were and be miserable, end our marriage, or seek help and figure out how to save our relationship. Divorce was never really an option. Even though it crossed both our minds, we were not giving up. We decided that our marriage was worth saving, and we believed that God would help us. We began by talking through some of our issues and being painfully honest with each other. We confided in a few of our closest friends and asked them for guidance and prayer. We were two broken people who needed fixing, but we had to humble ourselves to God and to each other.

Another helpful tool was reading marriage books together. We learned that women and men are completely different in how they think, act, and respond—and that's okay. Men and women have different needs and it's impor-tant to know what those needs are. We also learned how to love each other the way the other person needed to be loved.

We were taking small steps and we were making pro-gress. We knew we weren't where we needed to be, but at least we weren't where we used to be.

Change isn't easy. We found that in our marriage we had to come to the place to give up our "right" to be right and lay our pride down. We began to understand we are on the same team and if we were going to have a successful relationship, we needed to start cheering for each other instead of tearing each other down.

You might be saying to yourself, *Yeah, easy for you to say. I didn't have the family life that you both had. I don't even know what a healthy marriage looks like.*

Or you could be thinking, *But you don't even know what I have done to my spouse. My spouse will never forgive me. We are so far away from having a healthy, strong marriage.*

Ashlee: Pastor Joel Osteen preached a sermon a while back that has stuck with me. I am constantly asking questions, such as, *God, why would You want to use me? Why would You ever heal our marriage? The things I've done . . . the things I've said. I am not worthy to be called by You.*

Recently, I asked on more than one occasion, *Why, God, do You want us to write this book? We aren't biblical scholars or marriage experts.* And He always responds with, "I like to choose the weak because where you are weak, I am strong and I show up best in your weakness." And then I start thinking of one of Pastor Joel's sermons: "In the Bible, Jacob was a cheater. David had an affair. Paul was a murderer. Noah got drunk. Jonah ran from God. Miriam was a gossip. Mary was a worrier. Thomas was a doubter. Sarah was impatient. Gideon was insecure. Moses stuttered. Zacchaeus was short. Abraham was old. And Lazarus was dead."

So, why can't God use you? Why can't God perform a miracle in your marriage? Why can't those dry bones become alive again?

Let us ask you this question again, "Are you willing to do whatever it takes to have the marriage that you have always dreamed of?" If your answer is yes, in the following chapters we would love to share with you how we found the hope we needed to not just save our marriage, but to have a strong marriage and a continuing love affair.

GOING FURTHER

Following are some questions and talking points that we encourage you to read over with your spouse. Remember that you and your spouse are on the same team, and if your spouse wins, you win. Be as open and honest with each other as you can, always in the spirit of love and honor. It would be a great idea to compile these questions and answers in a separate notebook to refer to in the future when times get tough.

Talking Points

1. Are you willing to do whatever it takes to have the marriage that you have always hoped and dreamed of? If yes, sign and date.
2. On a scale of 1 to 10 (1 being deep in the valley and 10 being on the mountaintop) from your perspective, where do you each see your marriage?

3. Ask each other: "Is there one thing I could work on to make our marriage stronger?"

4. Would you each be willing to take a small step to add value to and strengthen your marriage? Set aside a few minutes a day for the next week to pray together as a couple. It can be short, but pray over each other, your day, your family, and your future.

The "Happily Ever After" Myth

When you stop expecting people to be perfect,
you can like them for who they are.

—Donald Miller, *A Million Miles in a Thousand Years*

Fairy Tales

". . . and they lived happily ever after!"

Ashlee: Fairy tales are some of the best stories because they leave you feeling all warm and fuzzy inside. Do you remember the fairy tales we used to watch and read as kids? I remember seeing the animated film *The Little Mermaid* as a young teenager and thinking how romantic it was. I couldn't wait to find my Prince Eric and live happily ever after. Most fairy tales end with the prince coming in to defeat the enemy, saving the day and riding off with the princess to live "happily ever after."

Many couples have the "happily ever after" mentality as they approach marriage. Everyone will come to the perfect ceremony and see the perfect couple share the perfect kiss before heading off to a perfect life. Don't forget about the perfect pictures, perfect cake, and perfect songs. It will be perfect from beginning to end!

Well, that's a great dream but doesn't factor in real life. Did someone take the time to explain what it will take to make that dream a reality? Don't get us wrong; marriage is amazing! Anything worth having is worth working on and fighting for!

During our wedding reception, an older man greeted us and said, "Wow! If every couple's marriage could start out like yours, there would be fewer divorces." We both stuck our shoulders back and had big grins on our faces, and one of us replied, "Thank you! We've been working very hard for many months to make this day special."

And man, did we have it all. We lit candles with our parents, we took communion together, we read letters to our parents thanking them for raising us in Christian homes, we had five songs played by a pianist and a flutist, we had three pastors pray over us. We even released doves in the air as Prince sang "When Doves Cry." Just kidding—but that song probably would have been a great foreshadowing of what was ahead for us. We had it all at our wedding. It was a Texas fairy-tale wedding, big hair and all. I remember thinking about what that man had said as we drove away, waving goodbye to our friends and family. I said proudly to myself, *Yep, we did it.*

A few years later, I thought about what he had said and felt a great burden of shame because I had started thinking about divorce. Especially at year five.

Soul Mates?

Many couples are just like us before their wedding days. All our time, money, and attention were directed toward the big day. We wanted to have the perfect wedding because we thought that if we started off on the right foot, then our lives together would be perfect just like in the fairy tales. We both agreed we were soul mates. We gave each other the tingles when we were with each other. "She makes my toes curl when we kiss." "My heart skips a beat when he walks in the room."

"Soul mates aren't born. They are created through the trenches of life." This is a quote we heard from marriage expert Jimmy Evans. We were attending a *Marriage on the Rock* curriculum training a few years ago, and when he said this a lightbulb came on. "Yes! Wow! That's so true!" we shouted quietly to ourselves. (Yes, that's possible.)

We constantly questioned ourselves during those early years.

"Did we make a mistake?"

"I'm not sure she is my soul mate. What if we chose wrong?"

"He gets on my last nerve."

"Soul mate? He's more like my *sour mate*."

We didn't choose wrong, but we certainly weren't each other's soul mates then. We hadn't yet been through any of the "trenches of life" together. There were times we felt like we were in the trenches of life—alone. Honestly, there were times we felt like we were in the trenches of life but were at war with each other. We were choosing to fight against each other instead of with each other.

———————

Ashlee: Just a few months after our wedding day, reality came crashing in. One day after washing my hands in our bathroom, I turned to dry off my hands on a beautiful hand towel with lace trimming that we had received as a wedding gift. I was proud of this hand towel because it was a luxury item we had put on our registry, and it was one of the few pretty things we had at the time. As I turned to dry my hands, it was nowhere to be found. It was a Friday morning and Clayton had left early to play golf with some friends. *Maybe he had washed it,* I thought. I looked all over our tiny house but couldn't find it anywhere.

That afternoon when Clayton got home, my excitement to see him quickly faded into frustration as I looked down to the side of his golf bag and saw what was once a gorgeous hand towel now covered in dirt. Not only was my prized towel barely recognizable because it was drowning in mud, but Clayton had put a hole in it to hang it off his bag.

"What have you done?" I asked.

Clayton assumed I was talking about him being gone all day to play golf and he barked back, "What are you talking about? I told you it was going to take all day to play golf."

"I'm talking about my towel hanging from the side of your bag with dirt on it!" I said. "And you put a hole in it too?"

He knew he had made a bad mistake and just put his head down while I continued to fume.

To say I was upset would be an understatement.

Then there was the fifty-five-gallon trash can he wanted to buy to put in the middle of our kitchen so he wouldn't have to take the trash out as often. I gave him a big no on that one. He told me that it had worked great with his college roommates. They loved it. I told him if he wanted a fifty-five-gallon trash can, then he could move back in with his college roommates.

I had my own idea of what marriage was supposed to be. I pictured it as a fairy tale in which Clayton would sweep me off my feet and romance me every day. I never imagined I would marry someone with issues I would have to live with for the rest of my life. I never imagined that the tingles would fade or that my heart would stop skipping.

We remember someone saying, "Your wedding day should be the happiest funeral you will ever attend because you have to die to yourself to have a successful marriage." That was something at the time I was not willing to do.

I wanted things done a certain way: The toilet paper down not up; the towels folded a certain way—and not used for golf; no commercial-sized trash cans in the kitchen. You know, the basics. Of course, I had my own hang-ups, too, that I wasn't willing to budge on. "A budget? I'm not living on a budget." "I know your mom is an amazing cook, but I don't like to cook and I don't want to cook."

We were so in love on our wedding day and were confident we were soul mates, but now we had these hang-ups neither of us were willing to budge on. How can soul mates have issues? Yes, they were petty issues, but during those first five years they grew into painful hurts that seemed unbearable.

Many people are searching for their soul mates but they simply don't exist. There are probably hundreds of people out there you could marry and be compatible with. Once you choose the person you want to spend the rest of your life with, then the work begins as you spend time in the trenches together. Becoming soul mates takes work.

Mike and Jennifer

When Mike and Jennifer first met, they weren't looking to make a connection. They went out with mutual friends for a fun evening and had no expectations of anything more. They were with a large group of people, but for some reason Mike and Jennifer just clicked. Mike woke up his roommate early the next morning to let him know that he had found the "one."

"I'm going to marry Jennifer!" Mike declared.

Jennifer was taken by Mike as well. She couldn't deny the mutual attraction. Shortly thereafter they began dating and soon found themselves in love. Mike didn't wait long to propose.

The wedding was going to be perfect and have all the extras. They were married on April 21, 2002. It was truly a fairy tale of sorts as these amazing people were convinced they were soul mates and that there was no doubt they were going to ride off into the sunset to the perfect "happily ever after."

Their marriage started out great, but slowly they began to have frequent disagreements that escalated into arguments. Communication was a new challenge for them. While dating it had been easy to talk to each other, but now a tension formed when they talked about certain topics. The honeymoon was over and they began to slowly descend into a deep valley.

Jennifer Told Us:

While we had some good times in our marriage and two beautiful children, we also caused each other a lot of hurt and pain. We weren't good communicators and when we would argue, we would spiral. Mike's words really hurt me emotionally. At first I would stick up for myself, shake it off, but through the years, it caused me to feel very insecure, lacking confidence, and beaten down. I was successful in my career, but I felt that I wasn't good enough.

Mike Told Us:

Sure, we had our challenges but nothing that we couldn't handle. We had it all. We had met, fallen in love, married, and had two wonderful kids. I would tell everyone around me how great Jennifer was as a wife and mother. The problem was that I wasn't letting Jennifer know how I felt and didn't realize how important that was to her. I thought she should know this and I shouldn't have to tell her.

———

August 2011 was a real downward spiral for their marriage. They were both so unhappy and were not getting along. Jennifer said she remembers one night suggesting to Mike he talk to someone or even that they talk to someone together. He said no, she needed to go by herself. It was from that point on that Jennifer's primary focus became her career, being the provider of the family, and being the best mother she could be. She convinced herself she needed to function within the dysfunction of their marriage. They continued to grow further apart and the arguing increased.

Finally, Jennifer had taken all she could and was longing for the attention that she wasn't getting at home. She needed a soul mate. As soon as the opportunity presented itself, she gravitated toward a relationship. It started out with someone showing her the attention she longed for. The relationship moved from an emotional to a physical affair.

March 15, 2012, their marriage was destroyed. Mike

discovered she was seeing someone else. He was devastated and heartbroken. They were at the lowest point of their marriage and didn't know where to turn for help. They knew they couldn't continue the way things were and that something needed to change. They separated.

Through all the hurt, resentment, unforgiveness, and marriage counseling, they desperately tried to work it out. Unfortunately, no matter what they did, nothing worked. They remained separated and were convinced divorce was their only option.

Every Sunday morning during that time, Mike took their kids across town to gymnastics. While surfing through the radio one day, Mike came across Pastor Joel. He heard Pastor Joel talk about the hope Mike was missing. In April 2013, after listening for several weeks, Mike decided to attend Lakewood Church.

One Sunday, after he returned home, he told Jennifer he wanted them to attend a service together and try it out. Maybe something there could help their marriage. Jennifer wasn't sure. After all, she didn't grow up going to a church like Lakewood. What would they do with the kids? Who would they sit next to?

Mike had an answer for each question.

Jennifer finally gave in and agreed to attend a service. She didn't know what to expect but she thought if she could endure it just one time, then Mike wouldn't ask again.

From the moment she walked through the doors, there was something different. Everyone seemed different. She felt something different. She wasn't quite sure why people were standing up and clapping with the music playing. It wasn't anything like she had grown up with. At the end of the service, when Pastor Joel asked if people wanted to rededicate their lives to Jesus Christ, she knew she had to stand. She began to weep and felt God's love as she had never felt it before.

That day was a turning point for Mike and Jennifer. They began to take some small steps that eventually led them out of the valley. It didn't happen overnight, but they continued going to church. They got involved in some marriage classes offered at Lakewood. Mike realized he needed to make some changes. He saw how important it was to uplift his wife and let her know what an incredible mother and wife she was. Jennifer knew she needed to change as well. One of the marriage teachers explained that love is not something we feel automatically. We have to choose to love and declare it!

The next day after hearing that advice, Jennifer woke up and, although it was hard to say, declared, "God, I am going to love this man today!"

The more Jennifer and Mike learned about God and marriage, the more they understood that God could bring restoration to *their* marriage and family. All they had to do was trust Him!

August 19, 2013, they renewed their vows at one of the Lakewood marriage classes and were on their way to becoming soul mates. Jennifer and Mike now have a thriving marriage and family, and we are honored to have them serve in the marriage ministry at Lakewood Church as incredible teachers.

I Can Change Him, I Can Change Her

Have you ever had the desire to help your spouse? Of course you have! There is something within all of us to help our spouses become the best they can be. After all, we can see our spouses' blind spots, and who better to help them change than us? They won't mind if we help by pointing out a few issues that we can see, right?

Clayton: On our forty-five-minute drive to work, I call my parents at least one time each week to keep in touch. This time, my mom picked up. We had our normal small talk and of course she wanted the latest news about her grandchildren. Then she began to tell me about some women from her local church who had formed a group. Ten women had begun meeting each week to pray for one specific purpose.

"We are coming together to pray for our husbands," she said. "We want God to change them!"

I instantly thought, *Oh no, what has Dad done now?*

My mom went on to say that she and the other women in the group wanted their husbands to become the spiritual leaders of their families. They were ready for their husbands to start leading their households in a godly manner, and they were willing to do whatever it took to see it happen.

After about three weeks, I reached out to my mom for an update on her prayer meetings.

She said, "Well, Clayton, it hasn't been going quite like we thought it would." She told me that they had gathered for one purpose but apparently, God had other plans. Mom said they had been blindsided. Each week they would get together and pray for their husbands, but God worked on each of them instead. She wasn't sure what she thought about the prayer meetings, but the ladies were willing to continue to meet until they felt like God was done.

As they met each week, God continued to work. Because of their openness to God, these women's hearts, attitudes, and lives were changed. Because of those changes, their husbands took notice and they began to change. God was honoring His Word: "Husbands . . . may be won over without words by the behavior of their wives" (1 Peter 3:1).

God honored the women's desire for change in their husbands but did it His way. He always gives us more than we can ever imagine, and He does it in a way where He gets the credit.

Great Expectations

We all have expectations about how things should go when we finally say "I do." You may not have liked what was modeled for you growing up, and so you made internal vows that your marriage would be different. Perhaps you cling to an image of true love from a movie and believe that could happen for you. The truth is, marriage is more than a fairy tale.

The Trouble with Movies

Movies seldom highlight the work it takes each day to have the marriage you want. Movies don't always elaborate on the benefits that come after the work either. Sure, they show us a beautiful wedding at the beginning and then go straight to "happily ever after." But what about the middle? Going through the trenches of life together are some of the best parts about marriage—how God brings two people to become one flesh through all the talking, the giving, the forgiving, and the loving that happens daily to make a marriage work.

Perhaps it's time to establish a new set of expectations for your marriage.

Maybe it's time to expect more from yourself.

As Pastor Joel says, "You can never control how someone treats you, but you can control how you treat that person."

When our actions reflect love, grace, and mercy, then we know we are on the right track.

Clayton: I remember one moment when I fell into the trap of thinking, *Well, Ashlee should know my heart.* It was a big mistake and became an eye-opening experience.

We were sitting in my office at church, while our ministry team was preparing for a big night when we were going to honor our volunteers. Time was tight, and we were still tying up loose ends. In the process of concentrating on the details, I neglected to tell Ashlee anything about our plans. I was feeling the mounting pressure of all the expectations and becoming overwhelmed. I assumed Ashlee knew this and would be willing to help. She always had in the past. On this occasion, however, I had not done a good job of keeping her in the loop.

I reacted badly when Ashlee asked, "So what exactly are we doing for the event Friday night?"

My thoughts were, *Are you kidding me? Didn't you read the e-mail I sent out with all the details?* I was so frustrated that I just blew her off and moved ahead, doing everything myself. What I didn't realize was that Ashlee wanted more details so that she could help me as only she could. Instead, I was short with her and basically ignored her question. I was completely in the wrong, but I didn't know it.

About five minutes after I refused to acknowledge her "absurd" question, one of the volunteer directors who served on our leadership team joined Ashlee and me in the office and asked, "So what exactly are we doing for the event Friday night?"

For the next five to ten minutes, I meticulously went over every detail of the night, and even asked if she had any suggestions for how we could make the night even better. She seemed satisfied with the details I had provided, said goodbye, and left.

As I turned around, Ashlee's face was a shade of red I hadn't seen before. "Are you kidding me? I just asked you that exact same question and you blew me off like I was nobody! Why would you do that?"

I had hurt her at her core and I hadn't even realized it.

That incident affected me deeply because I truly had not intended to hurt Ashlee. After that, I began to change my expectations of myself. My heart's desire was to do a much better job of showing grace and love to my spouse. I needed to make the choice to honor her every day if we were going to restore hope to our marriage.

The happily ever after can happen each day. Like the marriage teacher told Jennifer, love and happiness is not something we automatically feel every day. We must make a conscience effort to *choose it* and *declare it*!

Each day when we wake up, we need to begin our day by being thankful—thankful that we are alive, healthy, and whole. We must choose to be grateful for the spouse we married. We need to declare: "God I am going to love this man or this woman today!" and then trust God to do the rest. You might be one declaration away from the best marriage of your life!

GOING FURTHER

A great way to connect with your spouse would be to find a place, such as a local coffee shop, park, or restaurant, where you can take some time to talk through this chapter and answer the questions in this chapter's "Talking Points." Remember you are being intentional to learn, grow, and develop as a married couple. Just because you have been married for a while doesn't mean you should stop dating. We encourage you to plan a date night for this week. Put your phones away and invest in your future.

Talking Points

1. Ask each other what your expectations of marriage were before you got married. What did you each expect marriage to be like? How different were those expectations from reality? Take the time to answer and to listen.
2. Take turns sharing a time when you had expectations of each other that were not fulfilled.
3. Grab each other by the hand, look each other in the eyes, and take turns explaining five things about your spouse that you are grateful for.

The Right Choice

Love is patient and kind. Love is not jealous
or boastful or proud or rude.

—1 CORINTHIANS 13:4–5 NLT

We think sometimes that poverty is only being hungry,
naked and homeless. The poverty of being unwanted,
unloved and uncared for is the greatest poverty. We must
start in our own homes to remedy this kind of poverty.

—MOTHER TERESA

When you saw the title of this chapter you might have been thinking, "Oh good, a chapter I can read to find out if I made the right choice in the person I married." Well, that's not what this chapter is about. It's about, "Am I choosing to love my spouse daily?" We realized in the early years of our marriage that everything we thought about love was a little off. Love isn't based on a feeling or an emotional reaction to how you have been treated. Love is a choice, and it's a choice that we make every day.

If we are going to choose to love each day, we need to know and understand what true love is and what it is not. You can love something and not know how to use it. For instance, you could say, "Oh, I just love my phone," but if you don't understand how to use it, what good is it to you? Love is the response to understanding the value of something and the knowledge needed to care for it. We believe that successful marriages hinge on this knowledge.

"My people are destroyed from lack of knowledge" (Hos. 4:6).

"By wisdom a house is built, and through understanding it is established; through knowledge its rooms are filled with rare and beautiful treasures" (Prov. 24:3–4).

Unfortunately, we have witnessed the destruction of marriages because couples lacked this knowledge; but we also have seen many marriages restored and continue to thrive through the understanding of what true love really is.

Agapē Love

There are many Greek words used for the English word *love*. Some of these Greek words are eros, phileō, storgē, and agapē.[1]

Eros is a sensual and selfish kind of love. It's all about what makes me happy.

Phileŏ is a love that can change. You can always get new friends. It's an "if you're nice to me, I'll be nice to you" kind of love.

Storgē is a natural love or obligation, like the love you have for your kids or they have for you as their parent.

Agapē is a love that is unconditional.

In *Foundations of the Christian Faith: A Comprehensive and Readable Theology*, author James Montgomery Boice explains that, when the Hebrew Old Testament was translated into Greek and when the New Testament writers wrote in Greek, they found none of the common words for love adequate for conveying true biblical conceptions. They took another word entirely, one without strong associations, and used it almost exclusively. Because it had been little used previously, they could infuse it with an entirely new character. They created a word that would in time convey the type of love they wanted: agapē.

Agapē is a love that exists regardless of changing circumstances. *Baker Encyclopedia of the Bible* states that agapē means to love the undeserving, despite disappointment and rejection. And that's the kind of love God has for us. Regardless of what we have done or how we disappoint him, He will always love us.[2]

Jesus said, "A new *command* I give you: Love one another. As I have loved you, so you must love one another.

By this everyone will know that you are my disciples, if you love one another" (John 13:34–35, emphasis added). Jesus commanded us to agapē one another. The other types of love come naturally to us. Agapē does not always come as naturally because sometimes we are called to love the unlovable.

Jesus said to "love your enemies, do good to them, and lend to them without expecting to get anything back. Then your reward will be great" (Luke 6:35). How does God define agapē love? The most extensive definition is found in 1 Corinthians 13.

> Love is patient, love is kind. It does not envy, it does not boast, it is not proud. It does not dishonor others, it is not self-seeking, it is not easily angered, it keeps no record of wrongs. Love does not delight in evil but rejoices with the truth. It always protects, always trusts, always hopes, always perseveres. Love never fails. (vv. 4–8)

You may be thinking, "There is no way I could ever love like that!"

Don't worry. There is hope! The truth is, no one can love this way without Jesus at the center of his life. The Bible says that God is love, so it would be difficult to live by this definition if He wasn't a part of your life. With God, anything is possible, and that means He can help us love our spouses the way love is described in 1 Corinthians 13.

Love Is Patient, Love Is Kind

When we were first married, we thought we knew the definition of love. We assumed there were only two types of love. There was the love we had for our friends, parents, and family—phileō. Then there was the love we felt for each other—the goose bumps, sweaty-palms, and rapid heartbeats kind of love, eros. We were unknowingly missing out on so much. We hadn't yet experienced storgē, a parent's love for a child.

In the first few years of our marriage, we were clueless when it came to sacrificial love—agapē. To put each other's needs before our own wasn't on our radar. We tended to be selfish with our love rather than selfless. Patience and kindness didn't characterize our love. Even now, we continually make the *choice* to be patient with each other. In our conversations, text messages, and even in the ways we look at each other, we must *choose* to be kind. Sometimes it's challenging, but it's not impossible.

Love Does Not Envy, It Does Not Boast

During our wedding ceremony, when we stood nose-to-nose, it wasn't the beginning of a prizefight. We weren't two boxers standing before a referee getting our final instructions. We didn't go to opposite corners before the bell rang so we could come out swinging.

A wedding is a *covenant* ceremony that brings two uniquely gifted people together to become one team. It's a process. We will spend the rest of our married lives becoming one. If your spouse is with you and "on the same team," it makes it easy not to be envious of your spouse or to boast when something great happens for you. If you win, the team wins; and if your spouse wins, the team wins.

As you love your spouse, you become his or her biggest cheerleader. You are cheering for your spouse because you are on the same team. If your spouse wins, you both win.

Love Is Not Proud

Love chooses not to be proud. That's a tough one. When we become prideful, it means that we are already self-seeking.

Pride looks after number one and is inward focused.

Love looks after everyone else and is outward focused.

If there is one thing that can derail you and your marriage, it's pride. When you feel that you are right and your spouse is wrong, love says, "Who cares!" It doesn't matter who is right or who is wrong. Love chooses to look at your spouse and realize that he or she is on your team. Love chooses to give up your right to be right and submit to each other.

Clayton: As I have mentioned, every time I counsel a couple, I always begin by asking, "Are you willing to do whatever it takes to have the marriage you have always hoped and dreamed of?" And most of the time both partners say yes! But sometimes when I ask one or both, "Are you willing to change in this area?" I am shocked to hear, "No. I'm not."

"But you just told me you were willing to do whatever it takes to have the marriage you have always dreamed of," I respond.

One or both will say, "But not *that*."

Or one spouse is willing to change and do whatever it takes and the other spouse will say, "Nope. I have tried everything. There's nothing you can say that will help. I'm done."

I explain that pride is a destructive tool that is easily available and convenient to grab onto. The Bible says that "pride goes before destruction, a haughty spirit before a fall" (Prov. 16:18). When you are not willing to lay down your pride, you are setting the stage for destruction to enter your life and ultimately your marriage.

"Pride leads to arguments; be humble, take advice, and become wise" (Prov. 13:10 TLB). When we argue, how many times are we so sure we are right that we aren't even listening to what our spouses are saying? Ashlee and I can both say we have done that and it only made things worse. We now try our best to always choose love and to lay down our pride in all our disagreements.

The opposite of pride is humility. "Humble yourselves before the Lord, and he will lift you up in honor" (James 4:10 NLT).

Love Does Not Dishonor Others

Love does not envy, it does not boast, and love does not dishonor others. We never tear down each other in public and we don't do it in private either. As husband and wife, we are not only each other's biggest cheerleader, but we are also each other's biggest encourager. When you have been married for a while, it will be easy to find your spouse's flaws. The thing he or she did when you were dating that you thought was so cute, now it gets on your nerves. We are each painfully aware of our shortcomings and don't need help in pointing them out. We all want someone who sees our deficiencies and chooses to love us anyway.

Love Keeps No Record of Wrongs

Let's be honest, in any relationship we make lists. We may not write down our lists, but we have them stored in our minds. It could be a list of all the things we have done around the house. Maybe it's a list of things that we wish our spouse would help us with. Perhaps it is a list of all the things they have done wrong. It could also be a long list of defects we have discovered over the years in our spouses. Our gracious God gently reminds us that love chooses to keep no record of wrongs. Remember this amazing scripture. It's always good to burn our lists of wrongs. Keeping no record of wrongs and choosing to love your spouse is a daily activity.

A couple came in for counseling not long ago. They had been making some progress but it just seemed as though they would take one step forward and three steps back.

When one was doing well, the other was struggling. Then the tables would turn and it was the other's turn to struggle. We decided to bring them in individually and try to peel back the layers of hurt and resentment. We hoped to get to the root of the issue.

First, the husband talked with us and some things came up that were a little concerning. He said he needed to write down all the things happening in his head—everything his wife had done wrong throughout their marriage. He pulled out a journal in which he had begun recording his list. We were shocked but apparently it made complete sense to him.

We asked how this was helping him to become a better husband and how this journal was going to help his wife. Where was the journal with all *his* mistakes? Interestingly, he didn't keep track of his own mistakes in a journal; he kept those mistakes in his memory. We suggested it was time for him to make a better choice: to stop keeping track of his wife's mistakes and to become the husband she needed. To choose love rather than to keep a record of wrongs. That day God's truth shined on his mind and on his heart, and he began to make better choices.

Love Never Fails

We love playing games in our family. We love the laughter, the fun, and the competition that accompany them. We love all types of games—board games and card games. One card game we play is called Spades, a game you play with a partner against an opposing team. There are "trump cards," which are all the spades, thus the name of the game. In 1 Corinthians 13:8, God gives us the ultimate trump card when it comes to marriage—*love*. It says, "Love never fails."

God must have had marriage in mind when this scripture was written. He lists what love is not: it's not jealous, rude, or proud. Then He lists some things that love is: it's patient, kind, and trusting. One of the last things He says regarding love is that *it will never fail*. No matter how hopeless your situation, when you choose to respond in love, love will not fail.

Love Does Not Delight in Evil

We want to clarify that we truly believe there is hope for your marriage no matter how bad it may be, but we are not saying you should stay in an abusive situation, where you are putting yourself at risk of physical or emotional harm. In those cases, we recommend finding a safe place with family or friends. Set an appointment with a qualified pastor, church leader, or counselor, who can help guide you through the appropriate steps to begin the healing and restoration process. By taking some time apart, you are not admitting defeat for your marriage. Separation may allow you and your spouse to gain better perspective on your marriage and the steps needed for restoration.

Love Rejoices with the Truth

There is a level of vulnerability in every relationship. A marriage relationship is one place where there should be nothing hidden. Choosing to be open with your spouse about your past and your present is a part of love.

Some couples keep everything separate. Separate bank accounts and separate passcodes to computers, phones, and social media. Couples like this are keeping love from rejoicing in their relationship.

If marriage partners are playing on the same team, they should share the playbook with each other.

Love Always Protects, Trusts, Hopes, and Perseveres

A few years ago, when we were serving in our children's ministry, someone approached us with some pretty disheartening stories about one of our part-time staff members. They also shared some specific things this staff member had purportedly said. The information seemed a little off.

We had known this part-time staff member for many years and what was being shared didn't sound like anything the person would do or say. We had never heard the person use these kinds of words in any setting. The accusations weren't lining up with this person's character. Our doubts were confirmed a few days later when we discovered that the person sharing the misinformation had a personal issue with the staff person and was spreading untrue information.

Whether things are going well or things are going bad, it's a person's character that comes out. And love has character traits. When we choose love, these traits will come out.

Love always chooses to protect.

Love always chooses to trust and to hope for the best in people.

Love will persevere.

Love will remain when everything has been thrown at it.

Regardless of how we feel, when we choose to love our spouses in every situation, then hope will increase in our marriages. These characteristics will always remain true about love. When we choose to align ourselves with love, we get love's benefits. Suddenly we begin to protect and guard our spouses instead of tearing them down. Our trust and hope remain unraveled in the face of circumstances because, like love, we are persevering to the very end.

Do Everything in Love

"Be on your guard; stand firm in the faith; be courageous; be strong. Do everything in love" (1 Cor. 16:13–14).

To be on guard doesn't mean to be like a fighter with your gloves up, ready to defend yourself. It means to be fully awake, aware, and watchful. We are to be on guard and to stand firm while we are strong and courageous in whatever we might be facing. Then there are those last four words that encourage us to *do everything in love*. Everything? Really? Sometimes that can be quite a challenge. But remember, love is not based on *feelings*, love is based on a choice.

God promises us that love never fails. If we daily choose

to do everything in agapē love, then we can trust that love will never fail us.

Exercising Your Love Language

If you tallied up all the gyms where the Hursts have had memberships through the years, the total would be staggering. Honestly, it would be embarrassing. We have signed up for so many memberships with the best of intentions. Usually we sign up at the first of the year or right before swimsuit season. We tell each other that we need to get in shape. Typically, we begin with a burst of energy, believing we are going to transform our physical bodies with a new program and then we almost immediately find reasons not to go to the gym. After a few weeks we try again. None of our memberships lasted very long.

Looking back, we realize that our physical health is a lot like love. You can't be lazy with your physical health and you can't be lazy with your love. Not if you want good results. We made the decision that our physical health is important to us and because it is, we choose to work on it daily. We choose stairs over the elevator. We choose lettuce wraps over bread. We try to eat salads and healthy proteins every day because we are convinced that we need to focus on our physical health daily.

We have learned that the same thing is true for our love for each other. We need to work on our love daily. It's not always easy, but we purpose to sacrificially love daily. Thanks to Dr. Gary Chapman and his book *The 5 Love Languages*, we understand the importance of filling up each other's love tank regularly. His book also helped us identify the ways each of us show love and the ways we receive love. The five love languages are words of affirmation, physical touch, receiving gifts, acts of service, and quality time. Clayton's love language is acts of service and words of affirmation. Ashlee's is quality time.

Clayton's Love Language

Before we read *The 5 Love Languages*, I was always trying to do things around the house for Ashlee to show her I loved her. I would do the dishes, wash the clothes, and clean the entire house from top to bottom, waiting for her to tell me how awesome I was and how much that meant to her. She liked it at first and thanked me, but after a while she wouldn't say anything at all. In fact, sometimes it seemed she was annoyed that I did those things. It is important to understand I did all those things hoping to hear a thank you.

A simple acknowledgment of my hard work and her appreciation would have meant a lot to me. After she was introduced to the concept of love languages, Ashlee told me that doing all those things certainly didn't say "I love you" to her. Rather, it made her feel inadequate and that she didn't do anything correctly. She thought I did all those things because I believed she was incapable of doing them. I explained that I was doing them to *show* her how much I loved her and was hoping she would compliment me so that I would be assured of her love.

Truthfully, I was being selfish because I was showing her love in the way I naturally give it, instead of showing her love in the way she receives it. She told me she didn't care about any of that, she just wanted to talk. I was shocked!

Ashlee's Love Language

My favorite part of dating Clayton was our long talks on date nights. I will never forget our first date, which I was dreading. I was not wanting to date at the time, but reluctantly said yes when he asked me. After we sat down for dinner, he began asking questions about my family. Family was very important to him, so he told me all about his. He told me stories about his college life and had me laughing about things he had done both as a child and in college. Soon we were three hours into our date and still talking and laughing. I think we stayed out for another two hours just talking.

It was the best first date I had ever been on. And just about every date with Clayton after that was the same. I enjoyed talking to him, and I felt loved and cherished when he spent time talking to me. But after we got married, things changed. He came home from work and I was expecting those same kinds of long conversations during which he told me everything in detail, but that was not happening. He didn't want to tell me about his day. He didn't want to sit down and talk to me much at all. He was frustrated with all my questions. This made me feel unloved by him. After reading about the five love languages, Clayton realized that to show me he loved me meant spending time talking to me, really talking to me—without distractions.

Clayton: While I was dating Ashlee, I was trying to win her over. I recognized how much she loved to talk. I can picture her on our first date in that black summer dress and her face lighting up as she told me all about herself. When I won her as my bride, however, I thought there was no need to pursue her as I had when we were dating. I soon realized that the wooing needed to continue into our marriage until death do us part.

I realized that the best way to woo Ashlee was to fill up her love tank in the way she receives love. Even though spending quality time talking to Ashlee did nothing to fill *my* love tank, I knew I had to do it—and do it the right way—if I wanted to show her I loved her. If it was important to her, then it was important to me. I purposed to take her out on more date nights with uninterrupted time when we could talk about anything and everything. Our relationship began to get stronger and stronger as we intentionally focused on each other's needs.

Ashlee: I had to remind myself to thank Clayton when he did nice things for me and tell him how much I appreciated him. It didn't always come naturally to me, if I am being honest. I had to prioritize it because I now understood it is how he receives love. We went out of the way to speak each other's love language. And we overdid it a little.

I started writing Clayton little notes and leaving them in different places for him to find. I wrote about how much I appreciated everything he did for me. Sometimes I sent him e-mails saying how much I loved him.

Now we prioritize pouring love into each other's love tank on a regular basis so that when we need to make a withdrawal, we don't find ourselves in bankruptcy.

When we were growing up we had to learn how to balance a checkbook. We made sure to keep track of the checks we wrote and keep a running total of our balance. At the end of the month we would receive our statement, and we would verify which checks were outstanding and which checks had cleared. We always wanted to have enough money in our account to cover checks we had written. If there was not enough in our account, our check(s) would bounce and we would be in trouble with the bank and incur fees. Similar to bankruptcy, when you don't have the money to pay people you owe.

With any kind of account, including our love account, it's always important that our deposits are more than our withdrawals. We never want to bankrupt our love accounts. We always want to deposit more love than we withdraw.

Wouldn't it be wonderful if your spouse could give you the current balance of your love account? Sometimes your withdrawals may exceed your deposits, and frustration enters your marriage. The key is to continually be making love deposits into your spouse's love account.

"I'm bankrupt without love" (1 Cor. 13:3 THE MESSAGE).

If we keep our hearts open to the things of God and allow Him to fill us each day, then we will have plenty of love for ourselves and for others.

Thinking back to those first five years of our marriage, there is no doubt we were both bankrupt. Our love tanks were completely depleted and we felt utterly and completely hopeless. But God wasn't finished with us and He wasn't going to give up on us. He taught us how to sacrificially love each other. We *chose* to love regardless of the outcome. Slowly, our hope began to increase as we exercised our love for each other. Soon we could stand and walk out of our valley with the hope of never returning.

There may be seasons in your marriage when you feel that all hope is gone. As a couple who used to feel the same way, we want to encourage you that even though you may not feel the hope, it is always there.

Begin taking small steps each day and choose to exercise agapē love for your spouse. Before long you will begin making progress in your marriage and step out of your valley.

GOING FURTHER

"If our hearts condemn us, we know that God is greater than our hearts, and he knows everything" (1 John 3:20).

Do you believe in God and His Word? Then you must believe that God is greater than your heart. Have you had the following thoughts? "I'll never be able to love my spouse the right way." "Our marriage is hopeless." "Too much has happened for God to heal our relationship." Your heart is condemning you through these thoughts. Believe God's Word today and know that God is greater than your heart!

Talking Points

1. Name the different types of love. Which one is the easiest for you to give and which one is the hardest?
2. Take the *5 Love Languages* test at www.5lovelanguages. com. Ask your spouse to do the same. Make sure your spouse understands how you give love and how you receive it.
3. Each of you think of three ways you can show your spouse love in the ways your spouse receives love.

4

Love, Security, Respect, and Honor

Each one of you also must love his wife as he loves
himself, and the wife must respect her husband.

—Ephesians 5:33

When we honor someone we give that person a highly
respected position in our lives. Honor goes hand in
glove with love, a verb whose very definition is doing
worthwhile things for someone who is valuable to us.

—Gary Smalley

A Man Needs Respect and Honor

After reading many books and counseling many couples, we
have concluded that a man's number one need is *respect* or
honor and a woman's number one need is *love* or *security*.
These are typically at the core of every man and woman.

Respect: admire [someone or something] deeply, as
a result of their abilities, qualities, or achievements
(Webster's definition)
Honor: regard with great respect

When we started intensely working on our marriage, we
were given the book *Love and Respect* by Dr. Emmerson
Eggerichs. This book is based on Ephesians 5:33: "Each one
of you also must love his wife as he loves himself, and the
wife must respect her husband."

Ashlee: Dr. Eggerichs said that "husbands are made to
be respected, want respect, and expect respect." Honestly,
when I first read this, I was kind of annoyed by it. Why did
I need to show respect to Clayton? He didn't always deserve
it. Did this mean I just sit back and do whatever he tells me
to do with a "yes, sir" response? Well, to that idea I said in
my best Italian–East Texas accent, *"Fuhgettaboutit!"*

But as I read Ephesians 5, I realized that the apostle Paul
was describing marriage as a window into what the relationship with Jesus and the church is like, the husband as Jesus
and the church as His bride. Marriage is basically a metaphor:
a walking, breathing object lesson of how much God loves us.

When I think of honoring Jesus, it comes easy because I
am so grateful for everything He has done for me. I want to
pursue Him and learn everything I can about Him. Do I feel
like I fail Him sometimes? Of course! Do I show Him dis-
respect sometimes? Unfortunately, yes. But I know through
His grace and mercy He will always love me.

"How do I apply this to Clayton, Lord?" I prayed. "He's certainly not Jesus. He does fail me."

In my heart, I heard the Lord whisper back, "Honor him in everything."

"But God, he doesn't always deserve it. He is sometimes so rude to me. Or what about when he makes stupid decisions and I know it and I need to tell him so?"

The Lord replied, "Honor him where you want him to be, not where he is at."

Ugh!

"Okay, God, I will try this."

Men have an inner desire to succeed—in their jobs and especially in their families. Men need to know that their wives, above anyone else, respect them. Clayton told me he could handle anyone ridiculing him and saying harsh things to him—except for me. He said that when I ridiculed him or spoke harshly, it cut him to the core and he instantly felt like a failure. In fact, during our first five years of marriage, he felt so dishonored by me that he would spend more time at work than at home because he felt more honored there.

When he came home after work and wouldn't talk to me, I would start in with snide comments such as, "Well, I guess I will go outside and talk to the cows, they have more to say, thank you." Remember, we lived on a farm and we didn't have neighbors or social media during that time.

I would get annoyed when people at church would tell me how funny and outgoing Clayton was at work and how much they loved working with him. Several people said, "If he is like this at work, I can't imagine what he is like at home." I would just smile and laugh and bite my tongue and think, *Yeah, he's a big fat jerk!*

As I began trying to honor him, it wasn't always easy, especially when we were trying to come to a decision and we didn't agree. My first response had always been something like, "That's not a good idea. Why can't you see that?" But as I started honoring him, it changed him. He started rising to that place I desired him to be. He wanted to be home more. He talked to me more. The honor and respect I was now showing him caused him to cherish me more.

I also discovered that when I honor Clayton, it fills him with the confidence that he can do anything.

I'll never forget the afternoon of Christmas Day 2010. We were at my parents' house. My sister and I were watching a movie in the living room and all our relatives were in other rooms examining their new gifts. About an hour into the movie, I realized that I had not seen Clayton in a while. I asked my sister if she knew where he was and she said she thought she had seen him outside running. I was puzzled. Running from what? Clayton had never been one to go outside and run.

He later told me that while everyone was opening presents, he started thinking about turning forty the upcoming year and wanted to get in better shape. He had decided he was going to start running every day.

I laughed and said, "Okay, babe. Sounds good."

I didn't think much about it afterward, but when we returned home from the holidays, he continued every day with a running schedule. He was using the "Couch to 5K" app and was determined to run a 5K.

About two months after he started running, he had dropped quite a bit of weight and ran a 5K without stopping. I was so proud of him, but he didn't want to stop there. He told me that his new goal was to run in the Houston marathon in January the following year.

I looked at him and almost choked on my dinner.

"A *marathon*? How far is that again?" I asked.

"26.2 miles," he said.

"Do you run that all at one time? And you want to run this in ten months?" I asked, doubtfully.

"Yes," he said.

•I could tell my questions were frustrating him and I walked away.

About six months later, we were having dinner with some friends and one of them asked Clayton about his training for the marathon. By that time Clayton had registered and paid for the marathon and was diligently running every day. I, on the other hand, was concerned and still did not think it was such a great idea. He told our friend that he was registered, the training was going well, and he believed he would be ready.

I interrupted and said, "He does have the choice to run the full or half marathon. So, he could choose to run the half marathon if he wanted."

I glanced over at Clayton and he looked down but not before I saw the disappointment on his face.

Immediately I felt the Holy Spirit speak to me, saying, "You're right. Clayton will never be able to run the marathon, but it's not because of the lack of ability. It's because you don't believe in him."

That night when we got home I apologized for not respecting him. I told him I was 100 percent behind him and believed he could do it. Four months later Clayton finished the 2012 Houston marathon. Not only was I there, but I also invited some of our close friends to come and cheer him on. I had T-shirts printed with "Team Clayton" on them, and we made posters to hold up as he ran by.

It was challenging, but he said what kept him going was seeing all of us at each major milestone. He later told me that he never could have done it without me. He said everyone in the world could have told him he was crazy, but if I supported him, he knew he would finish.

Clayton: There is nothing more important to me than being treated in an honorable way. The opposite of this is true as well. There is nothing that gets under my skin more than being talked to or addressed in a dishonoring tone. Whether it is in the workplace or at home, honor is important. What's crazy is that I can't tell you why honor is so important to me, but it just is. After realizing this, I now appreciate even more how Ashlee chooses to show me honor whether I deserve it or not.

A Woman Needs Love and Security

Clayton: For Ashlee, security is as important as breathing. She constantly needs to be reassured that everything is going to be okay. Our relationship, our finances, our future, our kids, and the ministry we lead must be secure in her mind and heart daily. Insecurity in any area will have a negative impact on her. I don't completely understand why security is so important to women, but because I know it's important to Ashlee, it has become important to me.

While still trying to wrap my mind around this idea, I asked Ashlee, "Help me understand this. Is love more important to you or is security?"

Her answer set me back for a moment. "Clayton, I feel loved *through* security."

Ashlee feels loved when I sit down with her, give her my undivided attention, and talk through all the things she is concerned about. When we talk through issues, Ashlee feels secure and her concerns are put at ease. The security and love she needs come from getting answers to the questions that are important to her. I finally learned that this isn't a once a month or once a week discussion. This is something I try to do with her every day. When her needs are being met in this way, then she feels well loved.

When we sit down with couples to talk about their marriages, often we try to explain the importance of security. Usually the husband looks at us in disbelief and his wife bursts into tears. She has tried to explain her need for security to her husband and he didn't get it. Now hearing it from someone else, there has been a release of emotions and pressure that had been penned up for some time.

Not long ago we sat down with a young couple who needed some help talking through a situation. The husband began to explain something that had happened, something he viewed as harmless but had learned that it was eating away at his new bride. He told us that a few months before our meeting he had gone out to lunch with a female sales rep for his company. It had been strictly professional, but he had failed to mention it to his wife.

His wife explained that she is not the jealous type and the problem was that he never told her. She only found out about it a few weeks later because she saw a social media post to her husband from a woman she didn't know. It rocked her world. Her husband didn't understand that his wife's security had been shaken to the core—not because he had gone out to eat with another woman, but because he had failed to mention it. For weeks his wife lived in a constant state of insecurity, wondering what else he hadn't shared with her.

Ashlee looked at this young man and asked, "Don't you realize that security is as important to your wife as breathing?"

Then it happened. He looked startled and his wife began to cry. The husband understood for the first time the importance of security to his wife's mind and heart. He turned to her and, with tears in his eyes, apologized and acknowledged that he had messed up, and then he asked her forgiveness. It was something beautiful to see.

———

Clayton: A few years ago, I began to reflect on the year that was ending. I was setting some new goals and wanted to begin a list of prayer requests to track throughout the coming year. My plan was to list each request and write down when God answered it. Then I could look back at everything God had done in me and for me as well as have a record of all the things he laid on my heart to pray for.

One of the items I listed at the beginning of that year was something I heard the Lord telling me to do. I didn't hear it out loud, but he spoke deep in my heart. I wrote, "God, teach me to cherish Ashlee more than I did yesterday." I prayed that each day I would cherish Ashlee by putting her needs before my own. I didn't realize how much security this would provide Ashlee. As I cherished her, she felt more secure, which in turn filled her with love. What God laid on my heart to do for my wife had a lasting impact on both of us.

Ashlee: I have learned that although I need Clayton to provide security within our marriage, he can't be my only source of security. Jimmy and Karen Evans lead a worldwide ministry called MarriageToday, with a weekly program reaching more than 100 million homes. Jimmy said, "Your husband is a great Clayton, but he makes a terrible Jesus." When he said that, I realized that I sometimes find myself putting Clayton in this position—looking to him to meet all my needs and basically setting him up for failure because that's an impossible task and one only Jesus can fulfill. I usually find myself with these false expectations when I am not spending time with God.

Lessons from Astronauts

May 25, 1961, President John F. Kennedy gave a historic speech before a joint session of Congress. He told Congress that the goal of the United States would be landing astronauts on the moon within the decade and returning them safely to Earth. Tens of thousands of NASA employees were hired along with hundreds of thousands of contractors.[3] This became one of the biggest headlines of the decade. All eyes were on NASA and the men chosen to be astronauts. There was tremendous pressure on these men as they traveled to Florida for training and then across the country to promote the space program.

What happened to their marriages astounds me: of these thirty men, only seven remained married after their time in the space program ended.

Ashlee: I was shocked when I read that for the first time. I started researching the astronauts and their wives. One could assume that they led exciting lives. They all became instant celebrities. The men were pursuing their dreams of blazing the way into space and their wives were having tea with Jackie Kennedy and attending high society galas. I thought, *How exciting and fun! What could have gone wrong to destroy these marriages?* Lily Koppel wrote the following in her book *The Astronaut Wives Club: A True Story*:

> The astronaut wives were ordinary housewives, most all of them military wives living in drab housing on Navy and Air Force bases. When their husbands, the best test pilots in the country, were chosen to man America's audacious adventure to beat the Russians in the space race, they suddenly found themselves very much in the public eye. As her husband trained for every possible aspect of spaceflight, each woman had to prepare for the day when she would have to face the television cameras, when the world would be scrutinizing her hair, her complexion, her outfit, her figure, her poise, her parenting skills, her diction, her charm, and most of all, her patriotism. She had to appear calm and composed while her husband was strapped to the top of what was essentially the world's largest stick of dynamite, seconds away from being blasted off into space.[4]

Lily goes on to say that the wives couldn't turn to their husbands for help with these pressures because they were too busy training. Can you imagine the lack of security these women were experiencing? Not only were they bombarded with fame, but they didn't know if their husbands would come home safely each day. In addition, many of the astronauts were having affairs.

Astronaut Charlie Duke wrote in his book *Moonwalker*:

> With the work overload of trying to get a man on the moon by 1970, marriages were strained in the whole NASA community. There had never been a divorce in the astronaut office. After all, we were all-American guys—no one ever had any problems. It was thought that a divorce was death to your career and a chance to fly in space. But slowly and quietly the cracks were beginning to appear. I increased my efforts at work determined to do as good a job as possible and let my wife and family take a backseat. Little did I realize what consequences would come from that decision, and that the cracks forming in our marriage would bring us to near disaster.[5]

Charlie was the tenth man to walk on the moon, and after he left the space program he asked himself how he would ever top that. When he traveled to talk about what it was like to walk on the moon, he told his audiences that walking on the moon had been the greatest experience of his life. His honor was totally wrapped up in the space program, and his wife didn't feel loved by him and her security had been rocked. She became extremely depressed and even contemplated suicide.

Dotty wrote:

There were rumors of husbands running around on their wives, but we didn't talk about that. It was understood that divorce would ruin an astronaut's chance to fly, so indiscretions were kept discrete. Every wife had to deal with the knowledge that her husband was a hero and considered prize game by good-looking women wherever he went. Whether he was gone or at home, I felt alone. His career was the most important thing in his life, and I knew it.[6]

You are probably thinking they were one of the many astronaut couples who divorced, but theirs was in fact one of the seven marriages that survived. They explained in their book that when they both found Jesus and accepted Him as their Savior, that saved their relationship. Charlie wrote:

As the Holy Spirit began to speak to my heart about my sins, the burden of them did become intolerable. He said, "Charlie, the problem with your marriage is you. You don't love Dotty the way you should." I knew this was true. My love for Dotty had been dead for years. Now the Lord was telling me to love her as He loves the church. This was a 100 percent love. I repented and asked God to forgive me. I went to Dotty and told her I was sorry for all the troubles and problems and hurts I brought into her life, and that I was going to try to be the husband God wanted me to be. Then I ask God to help me love her the way he does. Together Dotty and I dedicated our marriage to the Lord. It wasn't instant, but God has resurrected a marriage and love that was dead.[7]

We cannot express to you how important it is for a man to love his wife in a way that brings her security and for a woman to honor and respect her husband. Ephesians 5:33 is the foundation for a strong marriage that lasts a lifetime. If you are in the valley of dry bones, this is your first step out of the valley.

GOING FURTHER

It is so important to realize that you and your spouse are both on the same team—if your spouse wins, you both win. Every man desires honor and every woman longs for security. When you wake up each day, try to think of ways you can show honor to your husband or provide ways to make your wife feel secure.

Talking Points

1. Ask your wife, "Can you explain to me why love and security are so important to you? Is there anything I can do to help you feel more secure within our marriage?"
2. Ask your husband, "Help me understand why honor and respect are so important to you. How can I help you feel more respected within our marriage?"
3. Share with your husband a time when he helped you feel secure.
4. Give your wife an example of a time when she filled you with honor and respect.

Effective Communication

Silence isn't golden and it surely doesn't mean consent,
so start practicing the art of communication.

—T. D. JAKES, *LET IT GO: FORGIVE SO YOU CAN BE FORGIVEN*

Processing Information

Communication: noun | com·mu·ni·ca·tion | a
process by which information is exchanged between
individuals through a common system of symbols,
signs, or behavior (*Webster's Dictionary*)

The way in which men and women communicate is so different. Sometimes the way we process information can be the cause of miscommunication and frustration with each other.

We have learned how important it is to ask questions about how we each process information. In asking these types of questions, you will start to gain valuable insight into how your spouse deals with the information they receive. The challenge is that it may not make any sense to you. Your spouse probably doesn't process information the same way you do, so it seems weird.

"Why do you think that way?"

"I don't understand why you would ever think like that!"

These are some of the things you might hear in our home when we are trying to work through a misunderstanding. We often have to reassure each other that it's okay if we don't process information the same way. What's important is that we are communicating.

The Number One Issue for Couples

As we began our new roles within the Marriage and Parenting ministry at Lakewood Church, we didn't want to assume that we knew what the biggest needs were in marriages. We knew that every couple and relationship would have its own hurdles. In our early years there were numerous issues we faced but the biggest one for us was communication. There wasn't a lack of communication but there was a lack of effective communication. So we set out to see if other married couples faced the same challenges.

Within the first few weeks of our new roles, we decided to do some research and e-mail more than fourteen thousand anonymous surveys to couples in our congregation. One of the questions on the survey simply asked to rank what each couple's greatest needs or issues were from greatest to least. Options included topics such as intimacy, communication, and finances. The response was shocking, to say the least. The surveys told us we were not alone in the struggle of communication. In fact, 98 percent of the surveys we received said that the number one issue in their marriage was communication! The remaining 2 percent must have been newlyweds because they claimed not to have any issues.

Different Styles of Communication

Clayton: When we were first married, to say that our communication was lacking would have been a severe understatement. We were so different in how, when, and where we conveyed information. Many times Ashlee would already be home at the end of the day when I finally arrived. There were times I would sit in the car for just a little while after getting home because I knew I was about to face an interrogation. It seemed that as soon as my key opened the door, Ashlee was there to greet me, always with a barrage of questions.

As a guy, my communication style was simple. I had always shared things in the same way I wanted to hear things. I would present Ashlee with the details in very quick and concise "bullet points." Ashlee, on the other hand, was all about the details. I mean *all* the details. Things like "Where did you eat today? How was the food? Why did you get fries instead of a salad? How did your food taste? Was it hot in the restaurant, because the last time I was there it was hot? Who all was there with you? What did you talk about? How did that make you feel? And how did they respond to that? What were their facial expressions *exactly*?"

Usually that was the drill and it was as if she asked all those questions without even taking a breath or without letting me begin to answer. It was so frustrating. I felt overwhelmed and I felt like a failure. I was having a hard time remembering all the questions she was asking.

As the questions flowed, I would start to shut down. It was almost as if I had become the star witness on trial and she was cross-examining me to see if my story matched up with the facts. We continued to live like this for years. There were days I didn't want to go home. I was tired and didn't have the energy to be ambushed with myriad questions. Ashlee felt hurt and abandoned because I would only slowly relinquish the facts of my day and refused to offer up any details. (Even as I write this portion of the book, she is adding in more details to this story.)

With time we realized that this type of communication wasn't effective for either of us. Ashlee understood that she needed to give me some time and space when I got home from work. I needed ten to fifteen minutes to just relax. That time gave me the ability to release everything I had been carrying that day.

I recognized that Ashlee wasn't putting me on trial. She really wanted to know about every detail of my day. She had missed me and wanted to feel as though she was a part of every experience I had that day. And I will be honest, there were days after I relaxed that I still did not feel like hashing out my day with her, but I also had to get to the point where Ashlee's needs were more important than how I felt. Meeting her needs each day was one of my top priorities, and communication was one of her top needs.

A Look Behind the Curtain

We had the opportunity to travel with some of the Lakewood staff to Australia. Our time there was life changing, but the fifteen-hour flight over was a different story. After we had been flying for a while, the flight attendants came through the aisles to pick up the dinner service. Then the inflight movie began (we were on an older plane that had TVs in each section instead of in front of each seat). We were a little disappointed we weren't on a plane that provided individual screens so we could choose what we wanted to watch, but we were happy there was a pretty good selection of movies. The first movie was an adaptation of *The Wizard of Oz* called *Oz the Great and Powerful*. After it was over, we agreed it was an okay movie and we were geared up for the next one to play as we still had about twelve hours left of our flight.

As the movie started we noticed that it was *Oz the Great and Powerful* playing again. A flight attendant checked into the problem and discovered that the airplane's entertainment computer was malfunctioning and could not figure out how to switch to another movie or how to stop the movie from playing. I think we endured that movie six more times before we finally landed in Sydney—and believe me, we never wanted to see that movie again.

There was one scene in the movie that replayed again and again in our minds. It was the one in which the characters finally see the truth behind the curtain and are shocked to realize that the all-powerful Oz was not the person they had believed he was. We discussed how similar it would be for married couples if they were able to look behind the curtain of their spouses' minds to see how differently from them they processed information.

After talking to many married couples, we have found that one of the most frustrating things in marriage is misunderstanding how or why a spouse thinks the way he or she does. Men often expect their wives to think about things the same way they do and vice versa.

We discussed what each other's brains are like and following is what we came up with.

Women's Brains Are Like Wires Behind a TV

Clayton: Ashlee told me that if I could "look behind the curtain" of her brain, I would see cables, wires, plugs, and connectors crisscrossing to every component. She told me it would be something like what I see when I look behind the TV in our entertainment center. Everything is connected and everything is plugged into a power source so that everything is on all the time. Each wire or cable represents a thought and these thoughts are constantly racing through her brain and can overlap. She is always thinking about something or about multiple things at the same time.

I would like to talk to the men about this description. You can visualize the mess behind your entertainment center, right? The wires crisscrossing back and forth making sure every component is connected to the other. I can picture the entertainment center in our home and there are so many wires and connections to every box, game, DVD, and TV. This is the perfect picture of your wife's brain.

Has your wife ever asked you a question that had nothing to do with the conversation you were currently in? In fact, the question had no relevancy to the last three conversations you had?

Ashlee asked me a question once and I finally got up the nerve to try to peek behind the curtain. I said, "Sweetheart, where did that question come from?"

I knew I might be in trouble when I heard her response: "Are you sure you want to know?"

She proceeded to tell me she had been thinking about something that happened last week, then that reminded her of something from college, which reminded her of a smell she remembered from her childhood. This went on for a while until finally arriving at the current question.

I was shocked! Behind the curtain of your wife's brain are wires that connect to everything from the moment she was born until now. And it continues to grow. That's why your wife asks you questions sometimes that have nothing to do with anything that is happening in the moment and she is expecting you to switch gears and have a conversation about this topic as easily as she can.

Men's Brains Are Like a Well-Organized Storage Facility

Ashlee: "My brain is simple and uncluttered." This is how Clayton described his brain to me. He told me if I were to look behind the curtain of his brain I would see a large, well-organized storage facility. Inside this facility are storage rooms and inside each room are boxes and each box is labeled with a thought or memory and none of the boxes touch each other.

"My thoughts don't lay on top of or touch other thoughts," he said. "Oh, and I have a favorite box."

"A favorite box?" I asked. "How do you have a favorite box? What does that even mean? Has it always been your favorite box? Is this box bigger than the other boxes? What color is this box?"

Before I got too far in my interrogation, he stopped me and exclaimed, "It's called the Nothing Box!"

"The Nothing Box?" I said, with a confused look on my face. "What is in the Nothing Box?"

Clayton paused for a moment and gave me another confused look and yelled, "Nothing!"

"How is that possible? You can't think about nothing," I said.

"Oh, yes, you can," Clayton grimaced and said, "and it's a wonderful box to be in."

"That's impossible!" I said.

"You know all those times you asked me what I was thinking about and I said nothing?" he asked.

I said, "Yes, and you were lying to me."

"No, I wasn't," he said. "It's the honest truth. I can literally think about nothing."

Ladies, I know you are thinking the same thing I am, that Clayton and your husbands are lying, but I have now read this in several books and have talked to other men who will concur that this is in fact true. Men can think about nothing. We have to take them at their word because it is absolutely impossible for us to do. This was such an eye-opening thing for me to learn. Many times I became frustrated with Clayton when he told me he was thinking about nothing. I used to think he simply didn't want to talk to me, and it hurt my feelings.

When Two Brains Collide

In general terms, every marriage begins the same way. Two people who are running their individual races choose to merge their lives. We decide to merge our friends, families, and life-styles. We are saying that we desire to merge *everything*. For some of us this is a great idea and there should not be any problems at all. In fact, we both assumed that the other would just see that our way was the best way and that would be that.

When we say the merging of everything we mean *everything*. There was a discussion at one point in our marriage about how we would fold our bath towels. This doesn't seem like a big deal, but when a certain way has always been your normal and someone wants you to change, it can be a little difficult. This may seem silly but we had a small argument on how we would fold towels. It seems insignificant now but it was a big deal then. It was as if we were staking claim to something significant and neither of us wanted to budge. After all, it would mean that our mothers folded their towels wrong, right? We didn't want our moms to be wrong.

This merging is like what we encounter when we drive cars. We can be going down a road and everything seems fine. Then we come to a yield sign and begin the merging process. There's give and take. If we don't give way to the other person, there will be a collision. Our marriages are a lifetime of yielding and submitting to each other. We *choose* to love each other and decide that the person is more important than the position.

How each of us processes information has provided some of the biggest opportunities for collisions in our marriage. Each of us have our "normal" way of processing information. Neither is right and neither is wrong, they are just different. Often we arrive at the same conclusion. But there have been times when we have become frustrated in trying to merge together toward a given issue. We have looked at each other and said things like, "I don't understand why you would think that way!"

One of us will look at the other and say, "It's okay. It's just how God made me."

There are times when our brains collide in that way. When this happens, we need to begin the yielding process and decide what is best for us and what is best for our family.

Strong Roots

Communication within a relationship is like the root system of a tree. The roots are the tree's source of water and nutrients. When a tree has a strong and thriving root system, the leaves and branches of the tree are healthy and whole. The root system also gives a tree its core of support when storms come. With strong roots, the tree may sway back and forth, but it won't break or be uprooted.

As we have pointed out, our root system early on was in bad shape. Our roots were primarily running on top of the ground. Our communication was all surface. We weren't open and vulnerable with each other. Because of the pain we caused each other, there were no tender moments that allowed us to go deep in our talks. We may have looked good from the outside but one good gust of wind would have toppled us.

Something was wrong, but we didn't know what it was or how to fix it. There were probably times where we didn't want to fix the problem. We assumed that everyone had the same issue and so we just had to put up with it.

God had so much more in mind than we ever thought would be possible. When we became open and vulnerable with each other, our communication grew stronger and our marriage got healthier. We began to love and care for each other.

Paul said, "Then Christ will make his home in your hearts as you trust in him. Your roots will grow down into God's love and keep you strong" (Ephesians 3:17 NLT).

God tells us what will happen with our roots as we place our trust in Him. We get stronger and we get a greater glimpse of the love God has for us. We believe the same kind of thing happens when you open your heart to your spouse. When we fully trust our spouses with the secret places of our hearts, our roots get stronger and our marriages get healthier.

Timing and Delivery

Effective communication is the secret to achieving a deep connection with each other. It's not something we are born with, but it's something that can be learned. It's also something that you should keep working on throughout your marriage. The better your communication becomes, the stronger your marriage will be.

We have become much better at effectively communicating with each other. Even though we are out of our deep valley, we regularly work on our communication skills. Sometimes we discover new ways to communicate and there are other times when we figure out how *not* to communicate. One of the best tips we can give you is to remember that successful communication always begins with good timing and delivery.

Clayton: I remember a Friday morning when Ashlee taught me the importance of timing and delivery. Our girls were off to school and we were relaxing at the house. Most Fridays we have the day off together since we work on Sundays and this was one of those wide-open days when we had no big plans. We had just finished breakfast and were enjoying our coffee. Ashlee took a deep breath and said, "Clayton, I need to share something with you, but I don't want you to get mad at me."

In a nanosecond, I had a choice to make. I could graciously receive what she was about to tell me or I could immediately put up my defenses. I had the feeling that I must have said or done something wrong. I paused, took a deep breath, and said, "Okay, I'm ready."

Ashlee began: "Well, remember last week when we went back home to visit our parents? There were times when we were at my parents' house that you responded rather harshly toward my mom. I don't think you meant to, but how you came across was mean and hurtful."

A part of me was hurt that she had to have this conversation with me to begin with. Another part of me hated that she felt that she had to set me up with the "I don't want you to be mad at me." But there was another part of me that was grateful. I was grateful I had a wife who loved me enough to point out one of my blind spots.

Ashlee could have immediately confronted me when it happened. Early on in our marriage we probably both had responded that way—too quickly. We would have pointed out each other's flaws in a much less tactful way. Fortunately, we have learned from some great resources and yes, also through our mistakes. We now realize that the job of husband or wife comes with the important responsibility of handling each other with great care.

As a spouse, you have been entrusted with the most intimate details of another person's life. It is important to guard and protect your knowledge. It can be challenging to lay down your pride and choose to be vulnerable. If you want to effectively communicate, the way you deliver sensitive information is very important.

Believe the Best, Don't Assume the Worst

We used to regularly fall into the trap of assuming what the other might be thinking. We didn't know if our assumptions were true or false. Regardless, because we made those assumptions, we didn't talk things through or ask questions. We thought our assumptions were valid.

Clayton: I remember times when I assumed that Ashlee had no feelings toward me at all. I reached that conclusion because I assumed I understood the meaning of certain looks or actions. My thoughts would grow and literally consume me: *Well, if Ashlee feels that way, then fine. Two can play that game!*

I remember having conversations with Ashlee in my mind. She had no idea about them because I didn't want to give her the satisfaction of knowing about the "arguments." They were so real to me then but I know now they had no value and in fact diminished our relationship. It made all the difference when I began having real conversations with Ashlee rather than those that took place solely in my mind.

Feelings are real—and powerful.

GOING FURTHER

Communication is the lifeblood of any successful relationship. Effective communication is critical to learning and growing. The longer you are in a relationship, the more intentional you should be in your communication. Each day make it a priority to work on how, when, where, and why you communicate. Don't make it a struggle for your spouse to gather information from you each day; instead choose to be generous and open with your communication.

Talking Points

1. On a scale of 1 to 10 (1 = lowest; 10 = highest), what score would you give your communication within your marriage relationship?
2. Ask your spouse for three things you could do to become a better communicator.

6

Healthy Conflict

Do all that you can to live in peace with everyone.

—ROMANS 12:18 NLT

In the long run, the sharpest weapon
of all is a kind and gentle spirit.

—ANNE FRANK, *THE DIARY OF ANNE FRANK*

What's Your Normal?

One of our favorite things about our job is providing pre-marital counseling for couples who are about to embark on the incredible journey of marriage. We love it so much because we want couples to know everything we wish some-one had told us before we were married. We obviously can't meet with everyone getting married at our church, so we also offer three premarital classes each week. We want to make sure everyone has a chance to get solid counsel before they are married. We are very passionate about this.

Conflict is one of the topics we deal with in counseling sessions or classes. Conflict between a husband and wife is normal, healthy, and should not be avoided. It is simply the process of being heard and understood. When you share your viewpoint with your spouse and he or she doesn't see the situation the same way, there is potential for that conflict to be handled in either a healthy or an unhealthy way.

When handled correctly, conflict in marriage builds character, and God constantly wants to build our characters. Your spouse is God's number one tool to make you more like Christ. Marriage reveals the things in our lives God wants to improve or change, and what better way to do that than by learning how to handle conflict in a healthy way? Some of the most character-building times in our marriage have been through learning to compromise in our disagreements.

If you were an engaged couple and came to us for pre-marital counsel, we would begin by asking about your parents and your home life growing up. Did you witness your mom and dad have conflicts? How did your mom respond? How did your dad respond? We find that for most couples, the two sets of parents handled conflict differently. But regardless of how different your home lives were, it was your "normal" growing up. When you marry and begin to respond in a different manner from what was normal for your spouse, there is potential for deep misunderstanding.

Ashley and Johnny

Ashley and Johnny are one of our favorite young couples we have had the privilege of taking through premarital counseling. When we began talking about healthy conflict, we laughed at the differences in how their parents handled conflict. Ashley's parents were extremely vocal and opinionated when she was growing up. She said her parents each had very specific views and were not afraid to share them heatedly with each other. She said it was her family's "normal."

Johnny's family, on the other hand, didn't discuss conflicts often. When his mother and father had a disagreement, it would quickly be swept aside and they wouldn't talk about it. He grew up seeing this modeled, and within his family it was what was normal.

Ashley and Johnny knew early on that conflict was going to be a challenge for them. They were learning how to work through it, but it had already complicated their relationship. We reminded them to offer each other some grace because they had had different "normals" for more than twenty years. We told them to never forget they were on the same team because it could take a while for them to figure out what healthy conflict would look like for them.

When an intense conflict with your spouse escalates to a place you never intended, your "normals" could be the culprits. Sitting down with your spouse and talking about what normal was for each of you could be a great starting place of understanding. Remember, this process builds character and that is exactly what God wants to do.

Your Response to Conflict

It is critical to have a reference point for what normal was for each of us but it's not all we need for healthy conflict. We also need to address how we respond to our spouses. The way we respond to our spouses will both give them the love and honor that they are longing for or can set us up for failure.

Ashlee: We were all created to respond, think, and act differently, so how could we possibly all agree on everything? I know for me, I was shocked the first time Clayton and I didn't agree. I thought, *Wait, why are we not seeing eye to eye on this? Why doesn't he agree with me? Why is he responding this way to me?* Our disagreements would go something like this:

> Clayton: I don't think we should do that.
> Ashlee: Why not? It's a great idea. We would save a
>   lot of money.
> Clayton: But we can't afford that right now.
> Ashlee: I know, but in the long run it would save us
>   money, and it's a really great product.
> Clayton: No. We aren't doing that. No!

(Clayton gives Ashlee a stern look. Ashlee runs to the bedroom and locks the door. She throws herself on the bed and begins to cry fiercely in her pillow. Clayton begins to pound aggressively on the door, demanding she open it. She says no, and he finally gives up and retreats outside to cool off. Ashlee then refuses to talk about it again and inside she is deeply hurt and frustrated with Clayton. Clayton doesn't understand why she won't talk to him and why she can't see that he is right. She starts to not tell him things to avoid a fight. He starts to make decisions about the household without her to prove that he can do some of this on his own.)

This type of scenario happened frequently in the beginning of our marriage. We wouldn't see eye to eye on something and then we would respond this way 99 percent of the time. Thinking back to the early days when something like this would happen, it was never over something big. Typically, the blowup was over something small and relatively insignificant. The conflict always happened based on our responses to each other. If the response validated what the other was saying, then the conversation went well. If the response was negative or sarcastic, then the conflict escalated and would quickly get out of control.

We finally had to sit down and talk through our responses. We realized that sometimes we responded based on what we had modeled for us growing up. Our responses were our "normals."

Clayton: For me it was normal to want to talk things out. I would always press Ashlee to get to the root of the conflict—to reduce it down, past the emotions, to uncover the real problem. I'll admit, most of the time it was probably me. Early on, if there was something I had been thinking about for a while, I assumed that Ashlee had read my mind and was up to speed with the conversation. So, I would usually be very short and abrupt in my responses.

A decision had been made and I was ready to move on and conquer the next issue. The challenge came when I would bring up an issue to Ashlee and she would immediately start asking questions. I didn't realize that I had done such a poor job of communicating with her. It probably came across to Ashlee that I was just telling her what we were going to do instead of asking for her input. At that point in our marriage, I certainly hadn't had the revelation that God had given me a helpmate.

For Ashlee, when a conflict would come up in our marriage, she would do just what the scenario describes. She would become frustrated with the conversation, because I wasn't ready to talk or have an open discussion, and she would head into the bedroom, locking the door behind her. Her idea of working it out was to ring the bell and retreat to our neutral corners. I would be yelling at her through the locked door, wanting to talk it out, but the damage had been done and she would begin to shut down. It was a recipe for disaster or at least for dysfunction.

We have learned a lot since those days. We have learned how to work through conflict together, helping each other along the way. We also realize there are times we are going to revert to the old way of responding. When one of us recognizes that is happening, we approach coming to a resolution in a very different manner. Our hearts are one now. We work through issues together. It's not about who will win or lose anymore. Over the years we have learned to submit to each other and God has done some serious character building in us. And He continues to build our characters through healthy conflicts.

A Monsoon of Disagreement

Ashlee: Preparing to teach on conflict at one of Lakewood Church's marriage classes, Clayton said to me, "We need a good story to share about conflict."

I replied with a smirk, "Well, why don't we talk about what happened last night?" He glared at me and said, "Really, don't you think it's too soon to pull that box out of the storage room?"

"We might as well talk about it now since we will be speaking on conflict soon," I said.

We both laughed but knew we were in for a challenging conversation as we recapped the events and argument from the night before.

It was a few weeks before our son Colton was to be born, and we were excited about our date we had been planning. It would be our last date before his arrival. We were busy at the church, having just launched the marriage ministry. We were also getting ready for our first marriage conference, which was only two months away. It was the perfect opportunity for a date night since both our daughters were going to be at sleepovers until the middle of the day Saturday.

Because of our busy schedule, we hadn't been able to spend needed time together and Friday night could not come soon enough. In Houston, a sunny day could instantly turn into heavy storms. And on this Friday, the sun quickly disappeared as the skies turned a dark shade of purple late that afternoon.

Clayton: I remember leaving the church that afternoon thinking, *It's going to take me forever to get home today!* For some reason, when it begins to rain in Houston, everyone behind the wheel of a car forgets how to drive. As I was heading home, Ashlee called to say she had already taken Addison to her sleepover because the weather was stormy. She already had Aubree's things together so all I needed to do was come home to pick up the two of them. Then we could be on our way to drop off Aubree and our date night could begin.

The plan seemed like a good one and we should be enjoying our evening out within the hour.

Aubree was attending a neighborhood friend's birthday party that evening. We were going to take her by the local mall to a party zone place and drop her off with all sleeping essentials and a birthday gift. I was thinking this whole thing through as I headed home. During the drive, I had spoken to the birthday girl's father and we had worked out where we would meet to leave Aubree in his care. Then Ashlee and I would be free to enjoy a romantic night out, which we both desperately needed.

Everything was going as planned until it started raining in a biblical fashion. About ten minutes before arriving home, it was raining so hard I couldn't see through the windshield with the wipers on high. I finally arrived home, changed clothes, and Ashlee, Aubree, and I jumped in Ashlee's car and headed to the party.

The closer to the mall we got, the harder it rained. Approaching the mall, I received a text from the birthday girl's dad telling me he was waiting at the entrance closest to the party zone. After Ashlee read the message, she said, "Hey, why don't you just take Aubree and her present in and we can take her sleepover stuff by later to their house? That way nothing will get wet."

I realize now this was a reasonable suggestion, but at the time I took it as a challenge to my planning. I said, "Sweetheart, I have it all planned out and we will be fine."

We went back and forth like this for a while and our voices were gradually getting louder and our responses were each getting a little more abrupt. Aubree was patiently waiting in the back seat, ready to go to the party, and I'm sure anxious to get out of the car and away from the dissension.

When we arrived at the mall, the rain was coming down like a monsoon. There was so much water! Ashlee tried one last time to help me see things from her perspective. "Babe, please, just leave her stuff, we can take it after our date."

I ignored her and clammed up, grabbed the umbrella, and got out of the car, slamming the door for good measure. As I walked around to the other side, Aubree told her mom, "Uh oh, Daddy is mad at you!" I grabbed Aubree, along with the birthday present and overnight gear, and headed toward the entrance. As I walked the thirty yards or so, my pants were soaked. I was wading through about eight inches of water, carrying my eight-year-old daughter, the birthday gift, all her gear, and the umbrella.

Drenched and struggling to hold on to everything, my pride still would not let me stop. Finally, I made it inside, put Aubree down, and began to scan the mall for her friend's father. I didn't see him anywhere and then realized I had pulled up to the *wrong* entrance. I had to walk Aubree to the other side of the mall to finally meet up with him.

When I got back to the car, I was exasperated with Ashlee, myself, and with my dripping wet clothes. Ashlee and I both knew we were past the point of successfully working through this issue, so we agreed to put the conflict "on the shelf." I placed it in a box and into one of the storage rooms inside my brain. Ashlee unplugged that wire.

Neither of us was ready to talk about what had happened and we both really wanted to go on our date. We had made a pact a few years before that if we were ever angry with each other and knew we needed some time before talking it through, we would put the issue aside and enjoy whatever was going on at the time. It took years for us to reach this decision. We had to learn to lay down our pride and always remember we were on the same team. It took a lot of maturing to get to that place. After we agreed to put aside this argument, we had a great evening out—my wet clothes and all.

The next morning, Ashlee said, "Why don't we talk about what happened last night? What was going through your mind that caused you to get so agitated with me?"

As we began to discuss what had happened, we realized that we had approached the situation from different vantage points and we hadn't shared our perspectives well with each other. I explained to Ashlee that I had spoken to the dad and had worked out a plan. Responsibility is very high on my list of strengths and if I tell someone I'm going to do something, you can bet I'm going to do it even if it means walking through eight inches of water.

Ashlee looked at me and said, "I just don't get why you are like this."

She was halfway laughing. I just smiled and said, "It's okay; it's just how God made me."

After talking through the good, the bad, and the ugly from the night before, we realized what we could have done differently. For me, it was all about laying down my pride. If I had done that, this situation would never have happened. A scripture I now look to for help in this area is Proverbs 13:10: "Pride leads to arguments; be humble, take advice, and become wise" (TLB). How many times are we so certain we are right that we aren't even hearing what the other person is saying?

Another scripture comes to mind. When I haven't treated

Ashlee the way she deserves, I try to focus on 1 Peter 3:7: "Treat your wife with understanding as you live together. She may be weaker than you are, but she is your equal partner in God's gift of new life. Treat her as you should so your prayers will not be hindered" (NLT).

Ashlee: I learned that sometimes even after talking through a conflict with Clayton, I am still not going to understand why he thinks the way he does and responds in certain ways. I still think it is crazy that he even argued with me about taking Aubree's sleeping bag and suitcase into the mall. Why could he not see how difficult that would be in a monsoon? I know he had made prior arrangements with the dad, but plans can change.

I have concluded that it's okay if I don't understand him sometimes. I know we will have future conflicts during which his viewpoint will make no sense to me, but I just need to be okay with that because our marriage is more important than a silly argument. Proverbs 14:1 says, "The wise woman builds her house, but with her own hands the foolish one tears hers down." One version says she tears it down brick by brick. I want to be a wise woman and bring strength and love to my house. I don't want to destroy my marriage brick by brick or one petty argument after one petty argument. My marriage is worth more to me than silly disagreements.

Song of Solomon 2:15 says, "Catch for us the foxes, the little foxes that ruin the vineyards . . ." It's those little arguments that over time can ruin a marriage. Lay down your pride and don't let petty conflicts poison your marriage.

I Would Rather Be Wrong Together than Be Right All by Myself

Clayton: Ashlee's older brother and sister-in-law have been some of our closest friends and confidants. I feel like I have known them my whole life. We were all married at young ages; they were married even younger than we were. Some people probably thought they would never make it as they were twenty and twenty-one when they married, with very little money, and a baby on the way.

Not long after they married, they knew they needed to reconnect with the one source that could bring them the help they needed. They both fell in love with Jesus and became involved in their church, which was my home church. We owe them a lot because they are the ones who invited Ashlee to church, which led to us meeting each other. As I got to know Jason and Staci, I very quickly became aware how completely opposite they are.

Jason and Staci

Jason, an introvert, would stay in his room for hours reading or on the computer gathering information during a party or a get together at their house. Staci, on the other hand, is an extrovert. You never have to wonder what she is thinking or feeling because she will tell you.

Jason and Staci's arguments during those early years mainly consisted of Staci complaining and Jason staring silently at her, unable to understand what had precipitated the argument or even to keep up with Staci's words. Jason had no idea how to respond. Their parents handled conflict very differently, but instead of taking that into consideration, they just continued in this unhealthy cycle.

I admit I was one of those people who was not sure Jason and Staci would make it. I wasn't necessarily thinking they would divorce, I was thinking more along the lines that one day she might just kill him. They have been married now for more than twenty-five years and have three adult children. They have learned over the years how to handle conflict in a healthy way by taking into consideration their personality differences. Staci taught Jason how to communicate with her, and he had to model for her that not everything is settled by yelling.

They still get upset with each other, but early on in their marriage they came to an understanding. Staci is an educator and a writer. She recently wrote a blog about a tubing incident during a camping trip to celebrate their son's high school graduation.

"Hey, babe. I think we missed our exit back there." I'm merely making an observation. My eyes search the river ahead. No more tubes to be seen. Confident and still completely reclined in the tube connected to mine, my husband looks cool as a cucumber. "No, we have a little way to go. I looked at the map last week. Don't worry." . . . As we continue to drift further and further along with other tubes no longer in sight, I can tell something is amiss. "Are you absolutely sure that we weren't supposed to exit with that last group of people?" . . . "If it will make you feel better, find your phone, call the rental place, and ask." I can't stop myself. I just gotta know. We are about to turn the bend, at which point the last exit will no longer be within eyesight. I dig my phone out of our waterproof container and call, only to hear an automated response. I begin to grow frustrated with my husband's continued laissez faire attitude, so I start paddling, trying to move us against the current, back towards the exit I can still see. Our tubes are connected, and there's an inflatable cooler between us, so my paddling is doing nothing but spinning us in place. The sun begins to set, and any sense of mindful relaxation exited with all the other river rats. Realizing the impracticality of trying to move our whole set-up by myself, I unhook my tube and try again, untethered. Progress! It's not fast, but I can fight the current much easier by myself. I make it about 20 feet and turn to see if he has yet come to his senses. Nope. He is still trying to get an answer on the phone. Furious, I begin paddling again. There's just no reasoning with him. If he has his way, we will both wind up who knows where, in the dark, and not even with the kids. He looks up. "You disconnected the tubes? That's not smart. We have to stick together." All of a sudden I recall a memory from very early in our marriage. We had come to a stalemate of sorts, both of us convinced that we were the ones in the right over something . . . who knows what. We had retreated to separate rooms in the tiny apartment we called home at that time. I was crying and wondering if I made a huge mistake, getting married so young. Our oldest child was already on the way, and I was feeling trapped and alone at age 21. Rocking on our bed holding my growing tummy, I remember realizing just how much I loved us—he and I together. I tried imagining my world without us. He was my best friend even though, in that particular case, I was still sure he was wrong. But that was no longer the point . . . You see? That night I had come to understand that I would rather be with him and be "wrong" together, rather than be "right" all by myself. It's become one of the bedrocks of our marriage: If his ship goes down, I'll be going down with it. No longer fighting the current, I make my way back to his tube rather easily. He hangs up the phone. "I'm sorry. I was wrong. We missed our exit," he says. For thirty minutes, we kick paddle, butterfly stroke, and maneuver our way back upstream to the final exit. It's not pretty. I will be so sore tomorrow. But we get to the landing, pull out our tubes and cooler, and make the march to our shuttle. And we did it—just like we'll do empty nest—together.

Ashlee: I just love what Staci wrote! "I would rather be with him and be 'wrong' together, rather than be 'right' all by myself." Our spouses are going to make mistakes. There is no getting around that. Sometimes we have to decide that even when we know our spouses are wrong, we are still going to be with them no matter what. When I don't agree with Clayton, I give it to God and trust Him to work out our differences.

My absolute favorite Bible verse is Hebrews 11:6: "[God] rewards those who earnestly seek Him." That has brought me so much peace, especially when Clayton and I are in conflict. I know if I trust in God and seek Him, I have a reward coming. Sometimes the conflict is severe enough that we seek outside counsel. And that's okay. We just make certain that we turn to someone we trust and who will truly be a mediator for us.

When dealing with conflict in your marriage, turn to the Word for hope and strength. "Cast your cares on the LORD and he will sustain you; he will never let the righteous be shaken" (Ps. 55:22).

The Power of Agreement

We have discovered that there is nothing more powerful than when we stand in agreement. The Bible says that when we are in unity or in agreement with each other, God commands a blessing. "How good and pleasant it is when God's people live together in unity" (Ps. 133:1). A few verses later, we are promised what will happen when we live in agreement: "For there the LORD bestows his blessing, even life forevermore" (Ps. 133:3). When we choose to submit to each other and live in unity, God promises us a blessing!

We want to encourage you to fight for unity within your marriage. Perhaps it's been a long time since you walked in agreement. There is hope because nothing is impossible with God.

Regardless of where you may find your marriage today, remind yourself of Ezekiel and the valley of dry bones when you face an impossible situation. Don't fall into a trap as we did. Declare how big your God is instead of describing how bad your situation is. We will always face challenges in our marriages, but our hope is found in the God who spoke galaxies into existence. His Word brings life and His desire is to make your marriage stronger than it's ever been.

When you keep Jesus at the center of your life, there is hope for your marriage!

GOING FURTHER

Remember the question at the beginning of this book? *Are you willing to do whatever it takes to have the marriage you always hoped and dreamed of?* You have to be willing to lay down your pride, willing to admit you were wrong, willing to take the high road and not let things escalate.

Talking Points

1. Did you ever see your parents have a conflict? What was it like? How did it make you feel to hear or see your parents disagree?

2. Ask your spouse, Is there something that I say or do that reminds you of my parents?

3. What are some things you can do as a couple to work through conflict together in a healthier way?

The Power of Partnership

Share each other's burdens, and in this
way obey the law of Christ.

—Galatians 6:2 nlt

The one thing I knew as a head coach was that I
couldn't do it all myself. My assistant coaches had so
much to offer and I had to empower them to utilize
their talents. Married couples need to do the same
thing and utilize the strengths of each spouse.

—Tony Dungy

When we made the commitment to enter a covenant
relationship with each other and God on our wedding day,
we had no idea what that would mean. There were times
when we felt like we were battling each other, but we now

understand that our battle is not against each other, it is against a common Enemy. Satan hates everything God loves, and God loves us and our marriage, so Satan is going to do everything in his power to destroy our marriage. He is our Enemy.

Operating on the same team started with small steps. For example, we stopped being sarcastic with each other. Our mind-set began to shift to being a team rather than seeing each other as the enemy. We remembered our vows to love, honor, and cherish each other for as long as we both shall live. To be honest, that was a little tough in the beginning, so we simply began anew each day.

Sometimes we would make small shifts and by the end of a day we both felt that we were a step closer to the marriage we had dreamed of. Some days one of us would make it and the other would fail miserably. We each had our share of bad days. We daily need to remind ourselves our spouse isn't the enemy. He or she is your helpmate, armor bearer, battle buddy, and teammate.

Craig and Samantha

About eight months before moving to Houston to join the staff at Lakewood Church, we met Craig and Samantha. Craig was the children's pastor at an amazing church in Southern California. They were preparing to uproot their family and move halfway across the country so Craig could become the children's pastor at Lakewood. They were excited about this opportunity for their entire family.

They arrived in Houston and began to put down roots. Craig immersed himself in his job at the church and Samantha was busy getting their two older kids settled and into their new school routines.

Things were beginning to feel like home when something shifted within their youngest son, Connor. Their once happy, playful son stopped making eye contact with them and was no longer forming words. After considerable testing, Connor was diagnosed with autism. Craig and Samantha were told he was on the middle of the autism spectrum. They were shaken to the very cores of their beings. They had no idea what God had in store.

Samantha immediately began to attach herself to Connor. He became her mission. She searched the Internet, read books, and investigated any possibilities of help for her son. Her world revolved around making sure she was giving Connor everything he needed to be successful. Samantha did all this for Connor, and at the same time made sure their oldest children, Cory and Courtney, were taken care of.

Samantha had a connection with Connor but connecting with his son was a challenge for Craig. He was trying to connect with a smile, a hug, or a verbal response. Craig told us it was so difficult for him because he was longing to reestablish their bond. Something he and Connor had shared was now missing.

Craig and Samantha didn't know how this would wear

on them as individuals and on their marriage. There were times when they felt as if they were heading in the same direction but taking separate paths.

They told us they constantly had to guard their relationship. Craig and Samantha had been married for many years but they had never experienced this kind of pressure and strain before. It was as if something or someone was trying to put a wedge between them. The faith cords that bound them together in marriage were feeling weak to the point of being susceptible to breaking.

In a family with a special needs child the divorce rate is higher because of the additional challenges. The pressure can be overwhelming, and if the husband and wife aren't able to come together and get help when needed, it can fracture the marriage. The emotional and psychological baggage is heavy. Often the father will leave because it becomes too much to handle.

Craig told us, "Samantha and I definitely had our issues, but the one thing we kept saying to each other was that we wouldn't back away. We would keep moving toward each other."

They determined that this setback would be a setup for something bigger for their entire family.

We have had a front-row seat to Craig and Samantha's journey. A long time ago they made the decision that regardless of what came their way they wouldn't fight their battles alone. They learned the secret of overcoming a potential valley season in their marriage is being open and vulnerable with each other. One way they have done this is praying together daily. They told us, "No matter what, we knew we had to come into agreement first with God and then with each other. There was so much power in our marriage when we learned how to pray together."

We first met Craig and Samantha in the summer of 2004 and we have become family over the years. God has been with them through highs and lows of marriage and raising kids. He has drawn them closer to each other as they have drawn closer to Him. They have raised some amazing kids while keeping their marriage strong through the process.

In 2008, with the blessing of the Lakewood leadership and the help of countless staff and volunteers, they launched the first Champion's Club for special needs and medically fragile children. Their hope and desire was to develop a program that would aid in the physical, emotional, and spiritual development of these kids.

Craig and Samantha are a dynamic couple advocating for these families. They have established Champion's Clubs in local schools, orphanages, and churches around the world. They have also established a nonprofit organization called the Champion's Foundation. Through it they offer curriculum, training, and devotionals to help families around the world. They would be the first to tell you that all this has happened through God's amazing grace and their decision to never fight their battles alone.

No relationship just stands still. You are either moving closer together or you are moving farther apart. In the middle of their battle, Craig and Sam made the decision to move closer together. That decision not only had a positive impact on their marriage but also on the lives of the thousands of families that have now been impacted through the Champion's Club.

"Remember the Lord, who is great and awesome, and fight for your families, your sons and your daughters, your wives and your homes" (Neh. 4:14).

We need to be on the same team, not fighting against each other but for each other. We do this with the sword of the spirit (God's Word) and the shield of faith. We need to speak out God's Word over our families and believe His Word to be true.

Two Are Better than One

Ashlee: The fifth year of our marriage, as we mentioned at the beginning of the book, was the year of our valley of dry bones. Because there had been so much hurt between the two of us, I had completely shut myself off from Clayton. I didn't share any of my personal thoughts or fears with him. After giving birth to our first child on October 17, 2000, my life entered a downward spiral. I didn't know it at the time, but I was suffering from severe postpartum depression.

I started having crazy thoughts like *What would happen if I put our daughter in the fireplace? What if I just forgot she was here and left the house without her?* I was also terrified to drive a car with her in it, so I refused to drive. On Sundays, Clayton had to be at the church very early, so I had a friend pick me up because I just knew if I drove something bad would happen. I was also terrified that Clayton was going to leave me and I would have to raise our daughter by myself.

I became extremely sick about a month after giving birth and had to stop nursing our daughter. I was heart-broken that I couldn't nurse her and felt like a complete failure. There were several women at the church who had given birth around the same time as I had. I remember sitting in the nursing mothers room during a church service and everyone was nursing their baby but me. I tried to find a chair in the corner and hide the bottle so no one would see. I sat there with tears quietly rolling down my face as these thoughts ran through my head: *What a loser! Why are you even in this room? You can feed a baby a bottle anywhere. In fact, anyone could feed your baby a bottle. She doesn't even need you.*

I was literally losing my mind. I was trying to fight this battle of depression alone and I was losing. Six months after giving birth I still felt like I was crazy. I cried all the time and the depression was exhausting. After a year of feeling like I needed to check myself into a mental hospital, I finally started coming out of it and feeling normal again.

And that's when there was finally a breakthrough in Clayton's and my relationship and we both began to fight for our marriage. As we finally started to share our hurts and to seek help, I began telling him about what I had been going through during the past year. I told him that after doing some research, I finally figured out that I had been suffering from postpartum depression.

Clayton felt so guilty.

He knew I sometimes said some pretty outrageous things and that I had seemed more fearful than usual, but he had just blown it off as me normally adjusting to motherhood. He also didn't want to ask me about it because he was afraid it would cause a fight. We cried together that night and he promised he would never let me struggle with anything alone ever again. He made me promise that I would always be honest with him about anything I was struggling with and allow him to be there for me.

Six years later, after our next child was born, I was fine. I had an easy pregnancy and delivery and she was an easy baby. She was our miracle baby. I didn't have any issues with postpartum depression, but Clayton would question me to make sure: "How are you feeling? Any weird thoughts? Anything I can help you with?"

Now fast-forward to eight years later. We have a beautiful and talented fourteen-year-old daughter, Addison, and a beautiful, servant-hearted eight-year-old daughter, Aubree. Our little family was complete—or so we thought. Early in the morning on October 15, 2014, I was having my quiet time and I was reading Luke, chapter 1, about when Mary visits Elizabeth and they are both pregnant. I had a weird feeling and thought, *I need to take a pregnancy test.*

I have no idea why that thought crossed my mind. We were not trying to have another child!

I told Clayton, "I know this is going to sound crazy, but when you go to the store, can you buy a pregnancy test?" He gave me the funniest look.

"Are you serious?" he said.

"I know. It's crazy, but just buy one."

When he returned from the store I took the test. Looking at the results, I screamed loudly enough that our neighbors probably heard me. Clayton ran into the bathroom and looked at me wide-eyed, his face a very pale white.

"It's positive!" I screamed again.

Keep in mind this was not a joyous scream; not like with our second child. I was in shock. This was not part of our plan. I was turning forty years old in two months. I was not going to have a baby. This could not be happening. I think I cried all day, all week, and possibly all month. We were past the stage in our lives for having kids. We were content with our family of four.

I was depressed for all nine months of the pregnancy and for months after the baby's birth. I had postpartum depression, pre-partum depression, forty-year-old-woman-having-a-baby depression. I had all kinds of depression.

Clayton sat down with me one day and said, "I know this is a lot, and I know you are thinking through a lot, but don't shut me out. Talk to me. I won't let you go through this alone."

So I let him in. I told him everything I was feeling. I

told him about how scared I was to have a baby at my age. At month four of the pregnancy we found out it was a boy. This baby now became even more real to me and I became even more terrified. I was in a dark place again, dark like year five of our marriage, but the difference was I wasn't alone. Clayton was battling for me with prayer and with love, and I had God going before me and speaking to me all along the way.

Let God Go Before You

Even though I was in such a dark place during my pregnancy, I didn't want my family to look back and think, "Oh, yeah. Mom was so depressed and cried all the time." I did everything I could to make it an enjoyable time for everyone, even though I was struggling to come out of the darkness. I planned a big gender reveal party with our family to celebrate knowing the sex of the baby. We had a family dinner at my parents' house and then we went outside to pop a huge balloon that was filled with blue confetti. When we popped the balloon, everyone cheered as their hopes for us to have a boy became real. As I cheered on the outside, I was still dying on the inside and afraid of having this baby.

After the gender announcement, everyone started thinking of names for him. I think our middle daughter, Aubree, wanted to name him Kristoff after the character on *Frozen*. Clayton liked my maiden name Hammer.

He said, "Ashlee, if we name him Hammer, he will for sure play football or at least some sport."

I laughed and said, "No, we are not naming our son Hammer."

I loved the name Andrew. Andrew means strong and courageous. And that's exactly what I needed right now—strength and courage. We already had three *A* names in the household and Clayton didn't think he could keep another *A* name straight. So we continued talking about different names.

On a Monday, Addison came home after school and said, "Hey, what about the name Colton?" We all seemed to like the name. No one had a problem with it other than Aubree who informed us that a boy in kindergarten who tried to kiss her hand was named Colten, but it was spelled with an "e" so since we were spelling it Colton with an "o" she said it would be okay.

After agreeing that we all liked the name Colton, I looked up the meaning online. When I learned that Colton meant "from a dark town" or "dark place," I thought, *No way am I naming him after anything with darkness in it*. I didn't want to be reminded of the darkness I was currently walking through. I prayed and asked Clayton to pray about what to name the baby because I wanted it to be something meaningful and to remind us of God and His promises.

That Wednesday night Clayton and I were at church and I was still struggling with what to name our son. I was feeling guilty about how I was feeling. How could I be so depressed about having a child when so many people were longing to have kids? I was a mess and cried all through worship. That night Pastor John Gray, an associate pastor and a dear friend, was preaching out of Isaiah. These are the words of God to His servant Cyrus:

> This is what the LORD says: "I will go before you, Cyrus, and level the mountains. I will smash down gates of bronze and cut through bars of iron. And I will give you treasures hidden in the darkness—secret riches. I will do this so you may know that I am the LORD, the God of Israel, the one who calls you by name. (Isa. 45:2–3 NLT)

Pastor John shared that as we allow God to go before us we will discover treasures hidden in the darkness. He said, "Some of you are in a dark place, but God wants you to know there are treasures hidden in that dark place." He said, "Some of you are even pregnant with darkness, but there is a treasure in there that is about to come forth."

I am sure that Pastor John meant spiritually, but for me it was both. I then heard God whisper to me, "Colton is your treasure; he's not your darkness." I started weeping and looked at Clayton, and he knew exactly what I was feeling. He knew because our relationship had become close and I had not allowed myself to go through this alone, he was walking with me.

Some of you reading this have been in a dark place like I was. Maybe you are in it right now and you feel lost, empty, and alone. You may be in a dark place that you feel you created yourself and you deserve to be in it. Some of you are there because of the pain someone else caused you. Let God go before you. Call on His name to heal your pain and discover the treasure waiting for you.

And don't go through it alone. Let your spouse in on everything you are going through. Have your spouse hold you accountable for your thoughts each day, and let him or her help you hold those thoughts captive through the love and power of Jesus Christ. Some of you might be thinking, *But I can't share these things with my spouse. It's too painful or shameful.* The longer you keep things hidden in the darkness, the more shame and regret you will have. God is light and where there is light, there can be no darkness.

June 11, 2015, we had our boy, Colton Hammer Hurst. (Yes, Clayton got to have the Hammer name in there. I guess we will see if Colton plays football.) I did go through some postpartum depression, but it was a much easier experience. Clayton kept me in check, asking me every day how I was doing and praying for me daily. I also prayed and asked God to go before me and help me through it. The crazy thoughts came, but I spoke to those thoughts with the power of God's Word. I kept my mind on His Word and spoke out His promises and I made it through.

Now we have this amazing treasure of a boy. Just this morning Clayton told Colton that we needed to pray before we left for the day. This boy loves to pray! As we gathered to hold hands he quickly tried to cram the entire cracker that he was eating in his mouth. With half of it sticking out, he looked up at me with his big beautiful brown eyes and smiled. He waited for us to bow our heads and then he bowed his. He stood there patiently through the whole prayer, waiting for Clayton to say amen. That is his favorite part because he likes to throw his hands in the air and yell "Amen!" and it is quite possibly the cutest thing in the world! He's our boy—our treasure!

GOING FURTHER

When we face difficulties, it is human nature to instinctively rely on ourselves to solve the problem. But the idea that we shouldn't be vulnerable and ask for help is absurd. Ecclesiastes 4:9 tells us that "two are better than one." One of your greatest assets is the person you said I do to on your wedding day. You should never allow your spouse to go through a battle alone or try to go through your own battle alone.

Talking Points

1. Ask your spouse to tell you the top three things he or she is concerned with right now.
2. Has there been a time when you felt as if you were all by yourself in a battle? If so, tell your spouse about it. (Remember, feelings are real.)

3. Describe what it would mean to you if your spouse fought for you the way you have seen your spouse fight for other things (for example, a job, friends, or family).

4. What are your spouse's greatest strengths? What are your greatest strengths? When you put your strengths together, can you see how God has put you together?

8

Forgiveness

He does not deal harshly with us, as we deserve.

—Psalm 103:10 nlt

When you cease to blame your spouse, and own
the problem as yours, you are then empowered
to make changes to solve your problem.

—Henry Cloud, *Boundaries in Marriage*

Ashlee: Does anyone really deserve forgiveness? I will never forget the first time I became extremely angry with Clayton. It's a story we often tell because it deeply affected my life. It was at this point I began seriously questioning God about whether I had married the wrong person because Clayton had done something so insane I didn't know if I would recover. We simply call this story "The Snot Story."

The Snot Story

We had been married for only a month when I began noticing something strange. There was something on our towels that would not come out even after they were washed. I thought maybe the laundry detergent was not completely rinsing out. Clayton was only bringing home a thousand dollars a month at the time, so we used the cheapest laundry detergent we could find. After taking a shower, we would sometimes hang our towels on the shower door to be used again before washing them.

One morning, as I was drying off after a shower, I felt something sticky all over my body. That same substance I had seen on our towels on other occasions was sticky and now was all over me. I grabbed another towel and dried myself off. I came out to eat breakfast and began telling Clayton about this mysterious stuff that I was finding in our towels and how it had rubbed off all over me. He slowly bent his head down, focused on his cereal bowl, and would not look up. I began to question his avoidance of eye contact.

Clayton finally looked up with a sheepish grin on his face and said, "Well, when I blow my nose in the tissues, they're too rough, so I started blowing it on our towels because they're so much softer."

I wish I could adequately describe how I felt at that moment. I went from shock to anger to confusion back to anger and stayed there. *"You mean to tell me that I just covered my body in your snot?"* I shouted. Did I mention that I was angry and still confused, but mainly angry?

What would cause a grown man to blow his nose on our soft, beautiful cream towels that had been a treasured wedding gift? But the even bigger deal was that *my body was covered in his snot*! I think I didn't talk to him for three days. I know it must seem silly, but this was our first big fight. He apologized, but I didn't accept his apology for quite a few days. I just could not understand why someone would do something like that, like for real. I still—I just can't.

Have you encountered something similar? Well, not your spouse blowing his or her nose on your towels, because I've never heard of anyone else doing that. But have you been in a situation where your spouse has done something that you just don't understand and you are hurt so badly there is no way you can forgive him or her? You think, *They don't deserve my forgiveness. You have no idea what my spouse has done to me.*

Without question, no one deserves forgiveness, but it is the goodness of God that sets the standard for our forgiving others. It's that *agape* love. It's that same love that motivated Jesus to willingly provide the ultimate sacrifice that allows us the grace for forgiveness and redemption of our sin. We serve a God who loves us so much that He provides forgiveness of not just the sins we have already committed but also the sins we have yet to commit. He willingly gives His forgiveness to all. What a God we serve!

Peter asked Jesus how many times we should forgive someone. He asked, "Seven times?" Peter wanted to know what the limit would be on forgiveness. But Jesus answered,

"I tell you, not seven times, but seventy-seven times" (Matt. 18:21–22). In other words, there should be no limit on forgiveness because when you don't forgive someone you are only hurting yourself. You're the one who suffers. I love what Beth Moore wrote about biblical forgiveness in her Bible study called *Living Beyond Yourself.*

> The Greek word most often used in the New Testament for forgive is Apheiemi. It means "to let go from one's power, possession, to let go free, let escape." In essence, the intent of biblical forgiveness is to cut someone loose. The word picture drawn by the Greek terms for unforgiveness is the means by which we securely bind ourselves to that which we hate most. Therefore, the Greek meaning of forgiveness might best be demonstrated as the practice of cutting loose the person roped to your back.

When we don't forgive, we are basically carrying that person and the weight of unforgiveness on our backs. This weight can put us in bondage spiritually, mentally, and even physically. We have known people whose hearts filled with unforgiveness destroyed their lives.

Forgive First

Clayton: Judah Smith, lead pastor of the City Church in Seattle, Washington, spoke at one of our services and shared something that powerfully affected us. He said when he and his wife, Chelsea, have a disagreement, they make it a point to see who can forgive first. It's become a game to them and the result is that unforgiveness doesn't have time to take root in their marriage.

When we heard about racing to be the first to forgive, it was a little challenging. We wanted to forgive but what if the other person didn't deserve forgiveness? What if what Ashlee said was really hurtful? What if she needed to suffer a little before I forgave her? (And Ashlee experienced the same thoughts about me.) There were times in our marriage when one of us would say or do something offensive, and it was around the tenth time to do it in a week. It was natural to think, *Obviously, [she or he] doesn't care about my feelings, so I'm not going to forgive [her or him] just yet.*

Sometimes I didn't mind losing the "Be the First to Forgive" game because Ashlee didn't deserve forgiveness. How else could I help her learn but to give her the silent treatment? (Ashlee felt the same toward me.) We were so messed up in our thinking. We willingly wanted and desired God's forgiveness, which we in no way deserved, but we weren't willing to unconditionally extend forgiveness to each other.

After Jesus told Peter to forgive seventy-seven times (Matthew 18), Jesus told him the story of a king who wanted to settle accounts with his servants. One man was brought to him who owed him ten thousand bags of gold. Since he was not able to pay, the king ordered that he and his wife and his children and all that he had be sold to repay the debt. The servant fell on his knees and begged him to be patient and he would pay back everything. The king took pity on him, canceled the debt, and let him go. The servant left the king's palace a forgiven man. He then found one of his fellow servants who owed him a hundred silver coins, much less than what he owed the king. He grabbed him and began to choke him. "Pay back what you owe me!" he demanded. His fellow servant fell to his knees and begged him, "Be patient with me, and I will pay it back."

But the man refused and had his fellow servant thrown into prison until he could pay the debt. When the other servants saw what had happened, they were outraged and went and told the king everything that had happened. Then the king called the servant in and said, "I canceled all that debt of yours because you begged me to. Shouldn't you have had mercy on your fellow servant just as I had on you?" The king then handed over the servant to the jailers to be tortured, until he could pay back all he owed.

Can you see what is happening here? The one who chooses not to forgive is the one who suffers the most.

Miguel and Laura

As the end of the year approached, our friends Miguel and Laura were evaluating their lives. Their marriage was a tale of two people heading down two separate paths, going in two different directions.

Laura told us that she had begun to pursue God with renewed passion and determination. Her heart was turned toward the things of God and she made the decision that whether Miguel was coming with her or not, she was going to run after God. She began the next year by reading the Bible daily and beginning and ending each day in prayer for herself, Miguel, and her family.

Laura recalled drawing closer to God than ever before. The closer she got to God, the more of Him she wanted. Her heart began to break because as she drew closer to God, Miguel was slipping farther away. Something was wrong and needed to change, and she knew it.

Laura told us that one evening her phone died and she asked Miguel if she could use his to call a friend. As she was trying to get into his phone, she accidently opened Safari and a search for pornography appeared. She was devastated. When she confronted Miguel, he denied it at first but soon after admitted that he had been looking at porn. She hoped it had been a one-time occurrence and asked Miguel if she could look through his phone. He reluctantly agreed and what she found confirmed her greatest fear. There was another woman. He had been making choices that could jeopardize their entire family as well as their marriage.

Through the tears and arguments, Laura had two thoughts repeatedly enter her mind: *I'm going to kill him* and *Call someone for help!* Fortunately, she decided to call some trusted friends and mentors at Lakewood Church.

Mary and Melvin, some of our long-time teachers, led

the marriage class Laura and Miguel attended. When Laura reached out to them, they immediately cleared their schedules to meet with her and Miguel. Laura remembers sharing the whole story with Mary and wondering if this would be the end of their marriage, if this would lead to divorce. Was there any hope for their marriage? Mary's response was full of love, grace, and forgiveness. She told Laura that God had a plan for their marriage in spite of these failures and disappointments, and she was confident God's plan didn't involve divorce.

As the meetings continued that day, they developed a plan to rebuild Laura and Miguel's marriage and restore their trust in each other. The plan involved counseling, accountability, and more. Mary and Melvin assured Laura and Miguel that they would be with them every step of the way.

The following Wednesday night, Laura and Miguel were attending a service, and God began to speak to Laura deep in her heart. He told Laura to forgive Miguel and let him know she would be fighting for their marriage. At first she was confused and thought whoever was making these suggestions was wrong. She thought, *Hold on, he should be asking me for forgiveness! This isn't right! I didn't do anything wrong. I'm the victim here!*

God wasn't swayed by Laura's thoughts. He continued to speak to her heart.

For the rest of the evening a battle raged in Laura's heart and mind. She knew that she knew that it was God telling her to forgive Miguel and fight for their marriage, but she didn't understand why. God's gentleness and love finally convinced Laura to do what He was asking. He was asking her to offer Miguel undeserved forgiveness. God was up to something bigger than Laura could see at that moment.

When they arrived home after the meeting, God continued to urge Laura to forgive Miguel. Before going to bed, she told Miguel what God had put on her heart and got on her knees. Laura told Miguel she forgave him. She finished by saying, "If you will tell me everything, we can start over."

Miguel was overwhelmed. He assured Laura that she knew everything. She believed him and went to bed knowing she had done what God had asked her to do.

Laura slept soundly, but Miguel was miserable. He had hurt the woman he loved and then when she got on her knees to forgive him, he had lied to her. God had used Laura to offer undeserved forgiveness and it had rocked Miguel to the core.

He couldn't take it anymore. He went around to Laura's side of the bed and woke her up. Miguel was a wreck, but God was doing something incredible inside his heart. He began to tell Laura everything—everything he had done during their marriage and everything he had done before, many things that Laura had never heard about. She remained unshaken in her attitude of forgiveness toward her husband. God had given Laura agapē love and His grace to forgive Miguel for his past, present, and future failures.

Today Miguel and Laura are some of our most faithful marriage leaders. God has completely restored and strengthened their marriage like they never thought possible. They willingly tell their story because their marriage is the result of undeserved forgiveness.

Forgiveness Requires Agapē Love

Charlie and Dotty

A fascinating part of the book *Moonwalker* by astronaut Charlie Duke and his wife, Dotty, is the recounting of how God spoke to Dotty about forgiving Charlie for all the times he had hurt her over the years. This happened not long after she had given her heart to the Lord. Within the first two months of becoming a Christian, she saw many prayers answered and began to hear God speak to her. He said, "You are beginning a brand-new life. You don't have to look back anymore. Your past is washed away, and you are starting a new life. Now, if you want your marriage to be born again, you must forgive Charlie."

Forgive Charlie? she thought.

She was convicted and defensive at the same time. How could she forgive all the times Charlie had hurt her? All the missed birthdays and the many times he had criticized her, plus the times he had flirted with other women—the list went on. She explained that Charlie hadn't asked for forgiveness and he didn't even think the things he had done were wrong.

She told God, "No! He doesn't deserve it. I want to let him suffer for a while. I don't want to forgive him."

She said God replied, "You can't call me Lord, if you don't obey Me. Those that call Me their Lord must do My will."

Dottie told God she would but didn't know how. God simply told her to agree to forgive Charlie and He would help her. So that's what she did. It wasn't always easy, but every time she remembered the times he had hurt her, she reminded herself of what the Lord had told her to do and to remember: "Remember, you have forgiven him, so it has been erased. It's not there anymore."

A wonderful healing took place as the Lord removed the resentment and unforgiveness from her heart. Through this healing, Dotty learned to love Charlie unconditionally. Before, she had loved him so that he would love her back. Now God was teaching her to love him 100 percent regardless of whether he loved her back or not. This is that agapē love we talked about in chapter 3. God told her that Charlie was exactly what she needed right now. What better way to learn unconditional love than to love someone who was unlovable.

Dotty began to do nice things for Charlie and to love him no matter what happened. After more than two years of loving him in this way, he agreed to go with her to a Bible study retreat. He thought, *She's been so understanding and patient with me, I should do this for her.* God became real to Charlie on that retreat, and on their way home he told Dotty there was no doubt in his mind that Jesus Christ is Lord. Dotty clapped her hands with excitement and told him that was what she had been waiting to hear.

During the following months, as Charlie began to get

a hunger for God's Word, the Lord began to speak to him about how to truly love his wife and the healing in their marriage continued.

Forgiveness Is a Choice

Forgiveness in marriage involves agapē love. Forgiveness isn't a feeling or an "ought to"; it's a "get to." It's a choice. Forgiveness is something we want for ourselves because we often believe we deserve it; however, it can be more challenging to choose to forgive our spouses. We may wonder if they deserve our forgiveness.

There are times we think that our spouses haven't done enough to earn our forgiveness. We are often quick to be the judge, jury, and punisher when our spouses are in the wrong. When we are the ones in the wrong, however, we expect immediate forgiveness. We judge others by their actions but we want to be judged by our intentions.

We should approach each day with grace and forgiveness for our spouses, especially when they don't deserve it. Then we have already forgiven them before they have made a mistake. This does not mean, however, that every day will be filled with "rose petals and rainbows." We expect there will be good days and challenging days but we determine to set our minds on forgiveness before getting out of bed.

Ashlee and I check our hearts each morning and decide that we will forgive each other before we start our day.

This mind-set does not mean we never make mistakes. But we *choose* to respond better. We choose to extend grace to each other regardless if it's deserved or not. We allow each other to make mistakes. Our hearts have changed but it hasn't happened overnight. It has been a journey during which we daily ask God to help us along the way.

GOING FURTHER

Choosing forgiveness is sometimes a challenge. When we are faced with something that seems impossible to forgive, God will graciously remind us of His willingness to forgive us. When everyone turned on Jesus as He was hanging on the cross for our sins, He forgave them and gave us the model to live by. You have a daily choice to make to forgive your spouse regardless of whether he or she deserves it or not.

Always strive to be the first to forgive.

Talking Points

1. Take a minute, just you and God, to see if there is anything in your heart that isn't settled with your spouse. If there is something, we encourage you to talk about it with him or her and forgive your spouse or ask for forgiveness. If you think it's too hard, ask God to help you.

2. How easy is it for you to forgive? Why is it so easy or why is it so hard?

3. Is there anything hidden away that you want to reveal to your spouse? With God's help, become completely honest with him or her. There is so much power when you can be in complete unity.

Sex Is Not a Four-Letter Word

Therefore, a man shall leave his father and his mother and
hold fast to his wife, and they shall become one flesh.

—Genesis 2:24 esv

Human beings are born into this little span of life of
which the best thing is its friendships and intimacies...
and yet they leave their friendships and intimacies with
no cultivation, to grow as they will by the roadside,
expecting them to "keep" by force of mere inertia.

—William James

The most intimate thing we can do is to allow the people
we love most to see us at our worst. At our lowest. At our
weakest. True intimacy happens when nothing is perfect.

—Amy Harmon, *The Song of David*

Shhhh . . . You Can't Talk About This

There was so much we wish we had known about sex before we got married. It seemed that everyone else had it all figured out but no one was willing to share the secrets of a great sex life within marriage. We knew our parents didn't feel like it was their place and there weren't any great resources available. We didn't understand that God had created sex and that it was beautiful within the confines of marriage. He gave us this gift but we weren't seeing it from His perspective.

When we were growing up, sex wasn't something you talked about. You never heard it discussed in a sermon. We would hear about it in our church youth groups but it was presented in a way that made it seem dirty, nasty, and warned you about it. We think our churches were doing the best they could with the information they had at the time. Of course, they were talking to a room full of teenagers with hormones ablazing.

Sex had become something like a four-letter curse word that you couldn't say until you got married. You'd better not say it, think it, or do it! Shhhh . . . it's a secret that you can't talk about until you get married, but when you get married, how do you talk about it?

It's in the Bag

Ashlee: When Clayton and I got married, we thought sex would be as amazing as it was portrayed to be in the movies.

I think he really believed that I would hang from a chandelier in lingerie, waiting for him to walk in the door from work every day. (We didn't have a chandelier. We lived in a little log cabin on one hundred acres, with cows surrounding us. Maybe he was expecting me to ride up on a cow in lingerie when he drove down our half-mile driveway that cut through a hayfield. I'm not sure.) I do think Clayton's idea of what sex would be like in our marriage was nothing like it ended up being.

I'll never forget a day about two months after our wedding. It was around 5:30 in the evening. Clayton was still working at a small Christian university in East Texas. I had cooked a big dinner for us—tacos, my specialty. (I was not much of a cook then and not so much now.) I was so excited to have a cooked meal waiting for Clayton. I heard our little car pull up and when I looked out our front window, I saw Clayton walking down the long path to our house, smiling ear to ear, holding a large trash bag behind him.

I was thinking, *What does he have? Oh, maybe he found a bag of money*. Living on one thousand dollars a month at the time was not so easy.

When he walked into the house he was so excited to show me what was inside the bag. "Honey," he said, "you will never guess in a million years what I was given at work today. It is going to save us so much money!"

Save us money? I thought. *Yes! Wow! What could it be?*

I excitedly looked inside the bag but quickly became both confused and alarmed. I slowly looked back at him. I then looked back in the bag to make sure I was seeing correctly. Then I looked at him and said, "You are right, I would have never guessed in a million years what was in this bag."

It was a garbage bag full of individually wrapped purple packets of condoms. That's right! Condoms! Twelve hundred condoms, to be exact.

"Babe," he said gleefully, "I went into the dean of students' office today and he had these boxes laying all over the place, and he was digging through each one. He told me that these were the welcome boxes for the incoming male students and that the vendor had accidentally put a condom in each. He then said he had no idea what he was going to do with all these condoms. And I said, 'I'll take them!' So, I ran and found a garbage bag and here you go!"

He handed me the bag as if he were handing me a dozen roses. I took the bag and looked inside again. Then he said, "Babe, these should last us like a year, maybe two—"

I quickly did the math in my head to calculate how many times we would need to have sex to use up these condoms. I concluded that I had married a crazy sex maniac.

The Past

Ashlee: My parents didn't talk to me about sex. It's not an easy subject to talk about. I will admit that I wasn't too excited to talk to my daughter about it. I have another daughter who I will have to talk with soon, and to be honest

I am not really looking forward to that conversation either. It's an awkward conversation to have. Honestly, the only time as a teenager I heard about sex was on television, the movies, or at church. The movies made sex seem super-romantic and intriguing, but at church all I heard was, "Wait. Wait . . . wait until marriage. No, no, no. It's so much better if you wait."

The problem is that when you are told no and to wait but not told why or what happens if you don't, you are left wondering, and sex is associated with shame. If you ask people who knew me growing up, they would probably label me as a "good Christian girl." I never really got into much trouble and, for the most part, I obeyed my parents except I was a little bit sassy at times. I liked being labeled a "good Christian girl." It was almost like getting a Girl Scout badge to sew onto my vest. I walked around proud I was that girl. Some would even say I was a bit of a show-off about it at times. (Not something I am proud of now.)

There was one secret about my past, however, that I never shared with anyone. I knew I had done wrong, but I also didn't want my "good Christian girl" badge taken away. I was sexually active as a teenager and it was some-thing I kept very well hidden. My justification was, *Well, I've never gone all the way, just to possibly third base, almost to home plate. That's not so bad.* But I might as well have slid into home plate because the secret scars of shame I carried were painful.

I had also given my heart away big time to one guy who

I just knew I was going to marry and so I thought, *What does it matter? I am going to marry this guy.* The end of my senior year he broke up with me and moved away. I was heartbroken.

As I moved on to college I held onto that shame and broken heart but just put it into a compartment in my mind and locked it away to hopefully become something I could forget about. During my college years I began attending the church where Clayton and I met. This was a great time for me as I discovered Jesus and His love for me on a whole new level.

Those years will always be very special to me because God's Word became alive to me for the first time and I didn't care about the "good Christian girl" badge anymore, I just wanted to learn everything I could about God's love. As I started my sophomore year of college, some friends said, "Hey, you need to meet this guy. He just finished college and I think you might really like him."

I was like, "Thanks, but no thanks. All I need is Jesus right now."

My friends didn't give up. They planned a game night at their house where we could meet. Anyone who has ever played games with me knows that would not have been the best way for me to meet a guy. I'm a little competitive. So, when Clayton walked in the door that night, I didn't give him the time of day. I was there to win. For some crazy reason, however, I think Clayton was attracted to my competitiveness and called me the next week to ask me out on a date.

This was before cell phones, so he called my house. I wasn't home, but my mom gave him my brother's phone number, where I was. Clayton called that number and my sister-in-law handed me the phone with a big smile on her face. When Clayton asked me out, I reluctantly said yes. Our first date was on August 5, 1994. We went out again the next night and the night after that. I think we saw each other every night for two weeks straight. He was like no one I had ever known. We clicked and had so much fun together. I quickly fell for him and was so happy he was someone I went to church with.

We began volunteering together in the children's ministry and any free time I had away from college was spent with him. Our passion started to get pretty hot and heavy. I loved kissing him and loved being with him. Our kissing soon led to other things. The compartment of shame that I had kept locked was opened back up again. We would serve at church and then go back to his apartment and passion would overtake us.

For our one-year anniversary we drove to Dallas to have dinner in a restaurant that overlooks the city and spins in a circle while you eat. It was very romantic. I bought Clayton a leather Bible with his name engraved on it because I so wanted our relationship to be built on our love for God, and in some way I thought the gesture would make the guilt a little less intense. But as we drove home from Dallas our passion couldn't wait the two-hour drive and we pulled over on the side of the road to make out—with the Bible right beside us—Lord help us!

As we continued our love affair I felt so guilty. I remember someone saying that Satan will do everything he can to get you in the bed before marriage and everything he can do to keep you out of it after marriage. And this was so true for me.

After we were married and Clayton came home with the bag full of condoms, I began resenting him and resenting sex. I felt so impure. As our communication began to decline, I felt like all he wanted me for was my body. I resented him for not being able to withstand the temptations before marriage and not keeping us to a higher standard. I secretly believed that God was punishing us for our impurity and that I would have to just endure sex for the rest of my life. And because sex had never been something that I could easily talk about, I never shared any of this with Clayton. I just silently resented him.

About two years into our marriage we attended a leadership conference with some other staff members from our church. After a session during which a female speaker shared her struggles with sex, I had a breakdown and confided in one of the leaders attending with us. I admired her a lot at the time because I thought she was perfect. I told her about my struggles during the past two years and the things I had done that I was so ashamed of. She asked if I knew what repentance was and I wasn't sure what she meant. She explained that I needed to get on my knees and repent of my sins. She also told me that she had done some things in her past that she was ashamed of and shared them with me, but she told me to never repeat any of it to anyone. She said there was no need to ever talk about my past with anyone ever again because I was forgiven and there was no need to think about it anymore.

I know her intentions were good, but not talking about it was the worst thing I could have done. I still felt condemned and I still resented Clayton, yet I never talked to him about it. He obviously knew something was wrong because sex for me had become just an obligation. There was no romance in it for me. I told him that when we had sex, the lights had to be off and there would be no talking. I had a "let's just get this over with" mentality. Also, because I was a pastor's wife, I was under the impression it was my duty to fulfill this need for him no matter what, so that he could be a better pastor. So I put up with it for eight years—yes, eight years.

After our fifth year of marriage, we experienced a lot of healing in our communication and in how we treated each other, but I still was not going to talk to Clayton about sex. I think the Enemy had closed my mouth on the topic for so long, I didn't even know how to begin to talk about it. Clayton even tried after year five to discuss it with me, but I just couldn't go there. It was too painful and I was so ashamed, but it was still affecting our sex life.

If you are not talking about your sex life, you probably don't have a great sex life. It wasn't until Clayton and I moved to Houston to work at Lakewood Church that I began to be honest with him. I began to let myself be freed from the pastor's wife persona I believed I had to fulfill. Well, I wasn't a pastor's wife anymore.

Clayton had been hired as the director of operations for the children's ministry. Also, the church was so large that I didn't feel like I was under a microscope anymore. I could just be me. During the worship services at Lakewood, God began to heal my heart as I cried out to Him and as I heard sermons on God's love, grace, and hope. I finally broke down one night in tears and told Clayton everything.

I told him about my past, about my anger toward him for not being the leader I needed him to be before we were married, and about all the struggles I had had during the past eight years. It was like a floodgate of grace poured out on me as I began to tell him everything. I told him how sorry I was for waiting so long, and how condemned I had felt. He just held me and cried. He apologized for how hurt I had been. We were both at a place of brokenness in our marriage that we had never experienced before. The final dried bones in our marriage were coming back to life again.

Sex is supposed to be a beautiful exchange of love between a husband and wife. And for eight years it had not been that for me. The wall I had built around my silent shame was so not worth what it was taking from me. Even now the Enemy still tries to use his old tricks on me in this area, but I just remind him that I am healed, I am forgiven, and I will never go back into that shame again.

Sex will always be an area in marriage that Satan tries to attack. Think about it. Satan hates us because God loves us. What is the example of Christ's love for the church in Ephesians 5? *A man's love for his wife.* What was the first institution God established in the Bible? *Marriage* (Gen. 2:24). What was the first commandment given by God? *Be fruitful and multiply* (Gen. 1:28 NKJV). (In other words, have lots of sex.) I believe it is Satan's goal to destroy marriages through twisting what the beauty of sex should be in a marriage. There have been many marriages destroyed because of adultery, pornography, or a sexless marriage.

If any of this resonates with you, don't stay behind that wall of shame. Talk to your spouse about it, pray to God to heal you of those deceptive wounds. You may need to seek counseling. Do something to get out of that place of condemnation and allow Jesus to pour out His beautiful grace upon you that will truly wash you clean of any shame.

Porn Is Real but a Lie

The multibillion-dollar industry of pornography is selling a self-gratifying lie. Pornography exploits women and portrays them contrary to real life. Men look at magazines or videos and assume that this is how a wife will look and act. She will always pursue her husband, never say no, and will always be in the mood.

Many men believe that sex's only purpose is their gratification. That is a lie. If you have struggled with porn or you are currently in the valley trying to get out, the best thing you can do is to confide in your spouse, ask for forgiveness, and then ask for help. Many men have successfully dealt with addiction to pornography. They broke free by the power of God and by partnering with their spouses to expose the Enemy's plan to destroy marriages.

So Different

We wish someone could have pulled us aside and explained all the differences between men and women before we got married. Not only do we talk differently and process information differently, but our wants and desires for sex are usually different as well. Men are more like jets and women are kind of like helicopters. Men will take off and climb to a cruising altitude, get to our destination, and then land. Women will take off and hover over to one area and then hover to another. Women don't typically go straight to their destination because they enjoy taking the scenic route.

With sex, men are usually ready before you can even say the word but for women it usually takes a little longer. Husbands think about their wives and sex many times throughout the day. Most women don't think about sex all day as their husbands do.

A man can have the worst day in the history of mankind and be ready for sex as soon as he walks in the door and his wife gives him the "look." It goes back to the storage facility. A husband can put his day in a box in a storage room and shut that door as soon as the opportunity to be with his wife presents itself. However, if a woman has a bad day and she comes home and her husband gives her the "look," she may have a slightly different response. Her mind is full of wires overlapping each other and plugged into the wall, thought after thought racing through her brain. She is thinking something like, *Really, tonight? Are you kidding me? You have no idea the kind of day I have had.*

A man can quickly put aside the issues of his day. For most women, it can be a challenge. A woman's day is intertwined with almost every moment of that day and possibly many days before. She may also have other things on her mind for later in the week. Everything needs to be settled in her mind for a woman to engage with her husband in the bedroom. It can also go back to a woman's number one need of love and security. If she doesn't feel loved by her husband, it can lead to problems in the bedroom.

Love languages also factor in. If a wife's love language is quality time and her husband hasn't spent time talking to her during which she believes he is listening, then it's harder for her to get excited about sex. If her love language is acts of service, then you could be one phone call away from sex after hiring someone to put shiplap on your walls. This actually happened yesterday.

Ashlee: My main love language isn't even acts of service, but when I told Clayton I would love to have some shiplap walls in our house (yes, we love *Fixer Upper*!) and he called to get someone to install it, I was turned on! Men need to understand that women aren't visual like they are. It's not about the way a man looks; it's about how he treats his wife. Don't get me wrong. I love it when Clayton looks super handsome in his gray Zara suit with that bow tie (yes, Lord!), but what gets me motivated for sex is when he talks to me and does things for me, especially things I am not expecting.

It's mostly about how a wife is doing emotionally. Often it has nothing to do with the husband's physical attractiveness, but everything to do with how the wife feels about him and herself and about the house and the kids and finances. For her it all ties together.

Open conversations about your sex life are imperative. The more open and honest the conversations with an attitude of healing and sacrificial agapē love, the better your sex life will be.

This information would have been helpful in the early days of our marriage. Men and women are different and that isn't a bad thing. Many times these differences are what God uses to mold us and make us into the people He desires for us to become. The challenge can be when we don't value our differences and then begin to resent each other because of them.

———

Maybe you have been married a while and you hoped that your sexual desire would increase to the level of your spouse's. So far it hasn't and you're feeling slightly defeated. Perhaps sex in the beginning of your marriage was great, but recently there has been a downward spiral. There is hope for you and your spouse in this area. Don't feel defeated or frustrated, but know that having open and honest conversations about it will help. Be bold. Create a safe place where each of you can share openly and honestly about your sex life.

It took a while for us to talk openly about ours. Once we began talking about our sex life, the weirdness faded. We learned to talk with openness, kindness, and respect for each other.

Let your spouse know what you like and what you don't like. Can you imagine if you nibbled on your spouse's ear thinking it would get them in the mood, but discovered it got on their nerves? Ha! That's what happened to us.

Never Stop Dating Your Spouse

We still date each other. We try to go on a date at least every other week. We take that time to really talk to each other. We talk about our dreams, what we love about our life, and anything else that is interesting to us and fun to talk about. It is not a time to talk about problems or issues with the kids or relatives. That can be saved for another time. We try to make our dates as romantic and fun as possible.

Sometimes we take turns planning the evening, keeping

in mind what the other one loves to do. We also plan a vacation each year for just the two of us. Some years we have taken amazing trips and other years the grandparents take our kids and we simply stay at home and enjoy our time together alone. After attending a vision retreat with Marriage Today, we now make time to do a vision retreat each year. It can be a getaway weekend or it can be done over one night, but we take time to get a vision for our marriage for the year to come of goals we have and what we want to accomplish for the year with our family.

Ashlee: You might be thinking, *What does this have to do with sex?* It has everything to do with sex! Because when a man takes the time to do retreat with his wife, what does that do for the wife? *It brings her security!* And when mama's needs are met by her man, then start playing the Marvin Gaye song "Let's Get It On"!

GOING FURTHER

The hope of having a great sex life begins with

- having regular, open, and honest conversations about sex,
- not being selfish,
- knowing your spouse's love language and doing something every day to show your spouse love, and being spontaneous and adventurous.

Talking Points

1. Schedule a date. Men, call your wife up and ask her out. If you need to find a babysitter, get one. Go wash the car and get ready like you used to. It doesn't have to be a fancy place but invest in her with your time and attention. Ladies, go get pampered and get dressed up for your man. Enjoy the night and make sure to plan a date night regularly.

2. Find a place where you and your spouse can talk openly and honestly about sex. Explain your likes and dislikes to your spouse.

3. Take the time to pray together about your sex life. Ask for forgiveness if it's needed. Remember that God created sex to be enjoyed by a husband and wife, so don't let Satan try to rob you in any way. Believe God to heal, restore, and strengthen your sex life.

Declaring Life over Your Marriage

In your unfailing love you will lead the people
you have redeemed. In your strength you
will guide them to your holy dwelling.

—Exodus 15:13

Success is not final, failure is not fatal: it is
the courage to continue that counts.

—Winston Churchill

One Step at a Time

Ashlee: One thing we have learned in twenty years of marriage is that a strong marriage comes from choosing to love the sometimes unlovable and choosing to move forward into healing and into the marriage you've hoped for. It took the first five years of our union to get there, but our prayer is that if you are not there yet, that God will accelerate your healing as you move forward together in His gracious love. You must first believe that God's Word and promises are true.

The Israelites in the Old Testament had this same choice to make. If they were to move forward into their promised land they had to believe God. Moses led the Israelites out of their captivity, out of their past, and out of the bondage they endured for hundreds of years (Ex. 14). While they were camping by the Red Sea after leaving Egypt, Pharaoh, the king of Egypt, changed his mind and decided he didn't want to lose them as his slaves. He sent his best chariots and officials after them.

As the Egyptians came closer to the Israelites, the people were terrified and complained to Moses saying, "What have you done to us by bringing us out of Egypt? Didn't we say to you in Egypt, 'Leave us alone; let us serve the Egyptians'? It would have been better for us to serve the Egyptians than to die in the desert!" (Ex. 14:11–12).

Moses replied, saying, "Don't be afraid. God will fight for you. You only need to be still" (Ex. 14:13, paraphrased).

But the Lord said to Moses, "Tell the Israelites to move on."

I can picture God saying this to Moses, and it makes me laugh. I imagine Him saying something like, "Why are you telling them to stand still, they need to move it? Hello, don't you see that their past is coming for them? *Tell them to move it!*"

Then God instructed Moses to lift his rod to create a path for the Israelites through the Red Sea.

I first read these verses during the summer of 2004 when I was doing a Bible study by Beth Moore called *Believing God*. I felt like I was in a place similar to the Israelites' and I had to make a decision—to stay where I was, to be still, or to move on. Since Clayton and I had come out of the desert time in our marriage, our relationship was thriving, and our marriage was growing stronger. In the winter of 2003 we both felt that our time in East Texas was ending and God was about to move us. We had no idea where that would be, but God had shared with each of us that we were going to move.

The only thing we knew to do was pray and trust God.

Clayton approached me one day and asked, "Hey, what do you think about driving to Houston one weekend and visiting Lakewood Church?"

I said, "Okay, but I hope you are not thinking that God is taking us there because I will *never* live in Houston. It's hot and the traffic is terrible." (Ha! I laugh at that now. It's funny how many times I declare to God that I will *never* do "that" and I end up doing that very thing.)

Clayton graciously said, "Okay, we won't move there, but let's just go check it out."

When we visited Lakewood a month later, we pretty much cried through the entire service. Everything Pastor Joel shared in his message was exactly what we had been sensing in our spirits about where God was leading us. We both felt a sense of peace. I knew God was telling us, "This is where I am planting you," and Clayton knew it too. So now the question was, How is this going to happen? Are they going to offer us a job today?

Of course, that is not how it happened. No one at Lakewood Church knew us. It's one thing to pray about a job you have been offered, it's another thing to pray about a job at a church where no one knows who you are. *And we are from little East Texas*, I thought, *a church of about one thousand members and we are expecting a church of thirty thousand members to offer us a job?*

Clayton and I began to pray, and when I say pray, I mean the face on the floor, crying out to God kind of prayers. We were believing to go somewhere nobody was asking us to go and thinking about leaving our extended families and all our friends behind.

During the next seven months we sold our house, moved in with Clayton's parents, and visited Lakewood every month. At the end of seven months, without any hint of an open door, we started thinking that maybe we had missed God's timing, so we bought a fixer-upper house and began the remodeling process. In the middle of our remodeling, Clayton received a phone call from Craig Johnson, the children's pastor at the time at Lakewood, saying that he wanted to meet with us in Houston.

Clayton was excited, but I told him no! I was done believing, we had just bought a house, and we were in the thick of redoing it ourselves. I knew God had spoken to both of us back in January that we would be at Lakewood, but I was tired of believing and nothing happening. It was our first big fight in three years. I had my mind made up that we were staying where we were. I remember Clayton pleading with me to take this step of faith with him and drive to Houston to meet with Craig. I said, "No! I'm not doing it. I've got to go. I'm late for my *Believing God* Bible study!" And I slammed the door and left. (Oh, the irony!)

I remember crying out to God during my drive to church, saying, "God, what are we supposed to do? I don't want to go. I don't want to do this."

At that week's Bible study, I heard Beth Moore teach on Exodus 14 in a little fellowship hall with a group of about thirty women. She told us how the Israelites wished they could go back when they were in between the Egyptians and the Red Sea, and how Moses said, "Stand still," but God said, "Go!"

Beth explained that the Lord asked Moses, "Why are you crying out to me?" (v. 15). She said sometimes we cry out to God, asking, "Lord, tell me what to do, tell me what to do!"

And the Lord says, "I have told you what to do and you are just waiting for a new answer!"

I thought, *Okay, God, I hear You!*

Beth said that when God gives us a word, He also empowers us to obey it. She said we need to hurry and obey. The longer we wait, the more that power wanes, and the weaker we become.

At the end of her message, she said, "If this is where you are at: a crisis of faith and indecision and you keep looking back and forth, but you know God is telling you to cross over and you want to make a commitment to do that, I want you to get on your knees now and I want to pray for you."

I was at the back of the room and instantly fell to the ground and began to weep as she prayed. I knew God was telling me to believe Him and to go toward our promised land. I went home and told Clayton what God had revealed to me during Bible study and that I knew we were supposed to go to Houston. I asked him to forgive me for giving up and not believing.

We traveled to Houston to meet with Craig in July 2004 and I began to pray and believe God again. In November Craig called Clayton and offered him a job in the children's ministry department and on December 30, 2004, on my thirtieth birthday, we moved to Houston to work for Lakewood Church. I am so glad I kept believing and moving forward in my faith.

I know it was our persistent faith that opened the doors to our promised land.

Move It!

Are you at a place of indecision in your marriage? Have you been taking steps of courage, but feel like nothing is happening? Are you thinking that you would rather keep things the way they have always been and stop believing they can get better? Or are you just sitting still, waiting for God to give you another choice? *Divorce? Could that be my option God?* That could be what you are thinking, but you know God has given you a promise about your marriage.

You might be reading this right now and your heart is beating fast and you know God is speaking to you. The promise God made to you about restoration for your marriage can happen, but you need to *move it*! You might be thinking, *But there are just so many painful things from our past that keep us from going forward. There's no hope.*

I want to share some verses from Exodus 14.

> Then the angel of God, who had been traveling in front of Israel's army, withdrew and went behind them. The pillar of cloud also moved from in front and stood behind them, coming between the armies of Egypt and Israel. Throughout the night the cloud brought darkness to the one side and light to the other side; so neither went near the other all night long. (vv. 19–20)

I love this! Did you see it? God was going before them, but as they started moving forward, God stood behind them to put Himself in between the Israelites and their past, their bondage. As you move forward with God and believe Him for your marriage, He will stand behind you and block the past with its bondage from getting to you.

Scripture goes on to say that God threw the enemy into confusion. When Satan knows that you are believing God, he gets scared because he knows the power that comes from believing God. Matthew 9:29 says that God will act according to our faith. Believe Him! Hebrews 11:6 says that He rewards those who diligently seek Him. As you believe Him, expect that reward.

That's what I had to do when we were believing God to come to Lakewood. Someone from our hometown told us, "Lakewood has thirty thousand members, why do they need you?"

I said, "I don't know, but I know what God spoke to us and that if I only believe and seek God, I have a reward coming!"

Even when I'm wrong and totally miss God, I still have a reward coming. His Word doesn't say He rewards those who choose *correctly*, it says He rewards those who *believe and seek Him*! What do you have to lose? Choose to believe Him, to believe for your marriage.

Get on your knees and make a commitment to God to *move forward* and pray the following prayer with your spouse. If your spouse isn't there or won't pray with you, then get down on your knees and believe for both of you.

Lord Jesus,

We believe You! We believe You are who You say You are and You can do what You say You can do. Go before us, God, and make a path as we move toward our promised land, as we speak to the dry bones to come alive again, and as we say to that mountain, "Move!" And we also ask, Lord, for You to stand behind us as well and block any attempt by the Enemy to destroy our marriage.

We speak to the past and to anything that has us in bondage and we say, "Move it!" And, God, we ask You to put that bondage into confusion as You did with the Egyptians so it won't even know how to attack us anymore and soon You will wash it away like You did when the Red Sea fell on the Egyptians. And we thank You, God, that in Your unfailing love You will continue to lead us and in Your strength You will guide us to Your holy dwelling, to our promised land!

Help us to choose to love each other every day until death do us part. We know with Your help and guidance we can have the marriage we have always hoped and dreamed of!

In Jesus' name, amen.

Identify Your Sackcloth, Remove It, and Clothe Yourself with Joy

Ashlee: I mentioned earlier how challenging it was for me to write on the topic of intimacy. I carried shame for so many years it was as if I was wearing that shame like a piece of clothing; almost as if I were Hester Prynne from *The Scarlet Letter*. Like she was forced to wear an *A* on her dress to shame her in front of everyone, I was forcing myself to wear a big *S* that stood for my shame and it kept me from completely going into my promised land.

When I first started writing that chapter, I was afraid I would have to wear that garment of shame again to write about those memories, but it brought me more healing because I was remembering from a place of restoration, and I was able to stop as I wrote and shout out to God and thank Him for gently bringing me through that time and not giving up on me.

Clayton and I were also able to talk again about that time and even more healing took place in our marriage. We shed tears, but our tears brought with them an even deeper level of intimacy. I relate so much to this scripture: "You turned my wailing into dancing; you removed my sackcloth and clothed me with joy, that my heart may sing your praises and not be silent" (Ps. 30:11–12). *Harper's Bible Dictionary* says, "A garment of sackcloth was uncomfortable and was therefore worn by those in mourning."[8]

I guess you could call them sad clothes. In Esther's time, no one entered the king's palace wearing sackcloth (Est. 4:2). If I had not finally taken off those sad clothes and opened myself up for healing, I would still be struggling in this area today. It would have kept me from entering the King of all kings's throne room and become completely healed. I wonder how many of you are thinking, *I want to move toward my promised land, but you just don't know what I'm wearing. It's painful and it goes deep.*

Could your sackcloth have a *D* on it for divorce? You may be thinking, *I love my spouse, but I just can't get over the fact that I have been divorced. I am so ashamed. I just can't move forward because I am so paralyzed by my past.*

We have some good friends who have an amazing blended family. They each have children from previous marriages, and they all get along well and love one another as if they were blood relatives. Their mom is always posting photos on social media of amazing parties she throws for her family and friends and of the exciting traveling they do together. She is one of the most loving and giving people I know. I'm sure most people would love to be a part of their family.

I was shocked when she confided in me that she was ashamed she was divorced from her first husband and that she wished she could have been married at this point in her life for as long as Clayton and I had been. I never would have guessed she felt that way. I said, "Are you kidding me? There are so many people who wish they could have the strong and loving family that you have. You are one of the most remarkable people I know."

It's amazing the lies we believe that Satan tells us. Most likely no one else was thinking those things about her, but because she believed them about herself, she was wearing that sackcloth.

Does your sackcloth have a *V* on it for victim? Were you victimized in your past and just can't get over it? I thought I was healed, but those memories kept coming back. As you decide to move forward toward your promised land, God will not only go before you, He will go behind you and protect you from your past. Any time those thoughts come at you, defeat them with the sword of the Spirit and start speaking out God's Word over those feelings.

Clayton: Could your sackcloth be an *A* for addict? Is your addiction to alcohol, drugs, or pornography just too much to escape? Maybe you have tried to walk away from it and it was just too difficult.

I was addicted to smokeless tobacco for almost ten years. For those ten years, there were times I was ashamed of the habit. I tried to hide it because I didn't want to be judged or looked down on by my family and friends. I tried to quit many times and I tried everything I heard about but to no avail.

Numerous friends encouraged me to stop; some even begged me. All the warning labels and even the disgusting videos shown in health classes didn't change my mind. There were times I felt like I had an *A* on my shirt and everyone knew. I even had a close friend who used the same tobacco as I did and, just a short time after his wedding day, he found a lump in his mouth. A few months later he had procedures to try and remove the cancer. Unfortunately, he lost his battle against cancer. I wish I could say that this made me quit, but it didn't.

I believed I was letting God down or that maybe He didn't love me the same as He used to. After trying everything, even running away from God for a time, I finally decided to run toward Him for the help I needed. I remember praying a simple prayer, something like, "God, please take this desire away so completely that even the smell will make me sick to my stomach." God graciously answered that prayer. Don't run away from God if you are dealing with an addiction, but instead run to Him just as you are! Just like that God removed my sackcloth of addiction and He can do it for you! God can heal addictions instantly or He may choose to work through trained counselors and programs.

Ashlee: Could your sackcloth be like mine, with a big *S* for shame? Has the shame from having previous sexual partners become too much to bear? Or did you have a baby outside of marriage? Or possibly you had an abortion and you think that God can never forgive you? In all these situations we need to say, "God, thank You for Your grace!" His grace covers a multitude of sins. And I can tell you right now that your sins, whatever they may be, are covered by Jesus' sacrifice on the cross. Walk in the full grace and mercy that God has for you. I sometimes felt as if my past had me stuck in quicksand and I was trying hard to escape but failed to look up to see that God was right there waiting patiently for me to take His hand so He could pull me out of my mess.

Clayton: Could your sackcloth be labeled with an *F* for failure? You have failed at your job or failed in taking care of your family's finances and have found yourself in major debt. Failure was something I wore at one point in our marriage. In a two-year period, we had amassed about twenty-five thousand dollars in debt. It was paralyzing. I was consumed with thoughts of despair. *How am I ever going to get us out of this? Where will the extra money come from?* Ashlee knew we had some debt, but she had no idea the amount and I wasn't about to tell her. I believed I had failed as a man, a husband, and a father. I was too prideful to ask for help. I was too prideful to admit when I messed up.

Finally I had to deal with my pride and admit to Ashlee that I needed help. At first she was devastated. But then she admitted we were both at fault. Something lifted when we came together and talked about our debt. We prayed and asked for God's help. We also determined to get out of debt and be done with it forever. We read books, looked up some great resources, and created a plan. For more than a year and a half, we cut back on everything. We didn't go out to eat or on a vacation. We turned off our cable, downsized to one car, and started telling our money where it was going to go. Something powerful happened when we worked together as a team and it felt like we could make it through anything. Ashlee helped me remove my sackcloth of failure and I've never been the same.

It's a New Day

Are you wearing multiple sackcloths that result in wearing a big *W*? You feel like you are just the *worst*. You can't do anything right. You yell at your spouse, you yell at your kids. You think terrible thoughts; you say things you shouldn't say. You just can't get it together. The multiple sins or hurts from your past have you too beaten up to move forward.

Today is a new day and a new beginning. Now is the time for you to take off the sackcloth and let God clothe you with joy. Let the joy of knowing God be the strength you lean on in times of struggle. "Because of the Lord's great love we are not consumed, for his compassions never fail. They are new every morning; great is your faithfulness" (Lam. 3:22–23). His compassion for us is new every morning. He is faithful to us and *never* gives up hope for us to heal.

Joel and Shawna

We were having lunch with our friends Joel and Shawna and they were telling us about their four children. They have two young adults and twins, a boy and a girl, who are in middle school. I asked Shawna if the twins were surprise babies like our Colton was. She said no.

She told me they had been trying to have children for a while and she had had a miscarriage. As she was having a sonogram, the technician became very quiet and called the doctor into the room. The doctor explained to Shawna that they couldn't find a heartbeat, that she had had a miscarriage and would need to have a DNC. She said she went home and went into her closet and mourned for hours.

Shawna told me that the way she remembered important times in her life was by keeping an article of clothing from that time. She kept the shirt she wore for her sonogram to remember the loss she had felt from the miscarriage.

With her next pregnancy, a year later she was back at her OB-GYN office when the technician could not hear a heartbeat through the fetal monitor. The technician called the doctor in. He explained to Shawna that there was no heartbeat, but he wasn't quite sure she had had a miscarriage this time. He wanted her to come back in a few days and have another sonogram. She remembered the painful loss from her previous miscarriage. When she got home she put on the shirt she had worn the year before during the sonogram and then went into the closet and began mourning as she had with her previous pregnancy.

As Shawna fell on her knees and tears began to fall, God spoke to her and said, "Take that shirt off and put on a new shirt. This is a new day."

She got up and obeyed the Lord.

Joel had been out of town and flew back home to be with Shawna for the next doctor's appointment.

As the technician was performing the sonogram, he made a sound, something like a "hmmm . . .".

Joel asked, "Can you not find a heartbeat?"

The technician replied, "I can't find one heartbeat—I have found two heartbeats!"

They were having twins. Double the blessing!

We believe God is saying the same thing to you as he said to Shawna. *Today is a new day!* His compassion for you never fails and it's new for you today. Stop wearing that sackcloth, whatever label it carries. Believe that God can heal you. The scars you bear from your past hurts or sins might not ever be erased from your memory, but when you can remember them without wearing them, then you are at a place of healing and believing God—you are at a place of restoration!

GOING FURTHER

In the fall of 2015, Pastor Joel released a life-changing book called *The Power of I Am*. In this book he talks about how powerful the words *I AM* are and the significance of what follows them. This book helped us to recognize detrimental things we would speak over ourselves. We stopped speaking those things and started speaking life.

We believe that within marriage there is power in the words *we are*. Declaring statements of faith over your marriage will cause hope to grow within each of you. Just as Ezekiel declared life over the dried bones, we need to declare, "We are restored," "We are going to choose to love each other," "We are overcoming our past," and "We are going to trust in God for our future together."

When you both make those declarations, among others, a shaking will begin to happen in your marriage, just as it did in the valley. There is power in your words. Never underestimate the power of "We are" and the blessings God will release over your marriage as you declare these statements in unity.

Talking Points

1. Identify one courageous step to take that you and your spouse can agree on to begin strengthening your marriage.

2. Do you feel like you have on a sackcloth from a past situation? Are you willing to lay it down so that you can put on what God says about you? Have you talked with your spouse about it so you can pray about it together?

3. Make a list of "We are" statements that apply to your current situation. Post that list somewhere in your house, and speak these statements over your marriage every day.

Jesus at the Center

*Trust in the L*ORD *with all your heart*
and lean not on your own understanding;
in all your ways submit to him,
and he will make your paths straight.

—PROVERBS 3:5–6

Never be afraid to trust an unknown
future to a known God.

—CORRIE TEN BOOM

We love weddings! A man and woman entering a marriage covenant with each other and with God is such a joy to witness.

Clayton: I have performed many weddings and at each

one there was always something that made it an unforgettable day for me. I have dropped the bride's ring during the ceremony. I have accidentally performed a wedding with a bright blue tongue (I have learned to never ask for a cough drop without knowing what kind before going on stage). At a wedding I performed recently, the best man got the bride's wedding ring caught in the lining of his jacket and as he desperately dug in his pocket, I frantically searched for some dialogue to keep the bride's mother from having a panic attack.

A Famous Wedding

Studying old Jewish customs, it's obvious they loved weddings as well. Wedding ceremonies covered many days and they were celebrations to be enjoyed by all. During one of these wedding celebrations recorded in John 2, Jesus' first miracle took place.

Jesus, His disciples, His mother, and the entire village of Cana had come to celebrate a wedding. It would last for many days and there would be plenty to eat and drink—or so they thought.

We can only imagine what Jesus and His disciples were doing at this wedding. They were probably, like most of the guests, sitting around enjoying the celebration. Perhaps talking about how God had brought together the young bride and groom. As they were enjoying the festivities, Jesus and His disciples could probably sense something wasn't quite right. Something was going on that would make this a memorable wedding. It could have turned out to be an embarrassment for the family putting on the celebration.

Jesus' mother, Mary, came up to Jesus and revealed the potential disaster. "They have no more wine!" Mary said (John 2:3). Notice she didn't ask Jesus to help. She just expected it. It's as if Jesus was in the corner of the room but Mary knew that His rightful place was at the center of this situation.

Jesus pushed back: "That's not our problem." In other words, we aren't responsible for this ceremony, so why do we need to be alarmed?

Mary's response was brilliant. Notice she still didn't give up after His first response. She didn't say, "Oh, well. I tried. He doesn't care." She brought the servants over and told them, "Do whatever He tells you!"

Jesus then had them fill up six water pots that each held twenty to thirty gallons. This water turned to wine.

This was Jesus' first miracle. A miracle that happened at a wedding. And a miracle that happened when Jesus took His rightful place at the center of the wedding.

Mary was demonstrating what we need to do not only on our wedding day, but also on every day that follows. We need to bring Jesus into the place of honor in *every* situation. We need to call on Him by faith to help, expecting results; and we also need to be prepared for Him to work miracles.

———

During our wedding ceremony, the pastor challenged us to each keep our daily time with God a priority. We knew that having a daily time with God and His Word had been important when we were single, but there was no way we could understand the magnitude of its importance when we were married. We soon discovered there is nothing more important than continuing to develop our individual relationships with God every day. Reading God's Word and talking with Him daily sets us up for success in our lives and in our marriages. Adding in a daily time in God's Word and prayer as a couple can revolutionize your marriage.

"Keep Jesus at the center of your marriage as well," the pastor told us. He knew something we didn't. He had first-hand knowledge he was trying to pass on to us. Although we appeared to be listening with understanding as we gazed into each other's eyes, we were clueless.

By the time we meet Mary in the second chapter of the book of John, it is clear she understood the magnitude of keeping Jesus at the center. We should all heed the same advice she gave to the servants at the wedding celebration that day. *Do whatever He tells you!* The servants had a choice to make amid the chaos. They could have thought, "Who is this guy and why should we obey this woman?"

Maybe they had tried everything else, so why not? Generations later we are grateful these servants obeyed. In the same manner, if we do what He tells us to do and we keep Him at the center of our marriages, then there will always be hope for our marriages.

Inside each of us there is a center place or a throne in our heart. We have the ability to put someone or something on that throne every day. Let's be honest, many times we decide we know what is best for us and we sit down on the thrones of our lives. We like the throne because we get to be the boss. We can quickly become *me* focused instead of *we* focused. When we put our own needs, wants, and desires in front of our spouses', then we are destined to have major issues.

Richard and Sheri

We have some dear friends who have learned over the years the importance of keeping Jesus at the center of their marriage. If you were to meet Richard and Sheri now, you would never guess the lives they lived before. In the beginning, Sheri attended church but Richard was the CEO of the church. That means he attended church at Christmas, Easter, and other major holidays. Each were raising kids from previous marriages that had unfortunately failed. They had decided that if they did meet another person they liked, marriage was off the table. They had been there and done that, and they decided it just wasn't for them.

The first time they met was at the beach with some mutual friends. Sheri told Richard that she was a successful Mary Kay director with a new car that was the result of her accomplishments. What she didn't tell him was that her business was tanking and she had already been contacted about giving the car back. Richard was spinning some half-truths as well when he told Sheri he had a growing construction business. Sheri was thrilled and thought she had finally met her sugar-daddy! Richard was excited and thought he wouldn't have to explain his business because he thought he had found his sugar-momma. They were both living paycheck to paycheck and had no intentions of marrying again. So they moved in together.

They experienced a lot of anxiety and fear as they merged their two families. Their blended family had lots of ups and down but never a dull moment. When the kids were away, Richard would use drugs and alcohol to ease the pain of the reality invading their lives. Sheri used the drugs and alcohol to connect with and please Richard. After years of trying to be happy and fulfilled, they realized something was missing. They became so unhappy that they became destructive toward each other. Richard was so angry at Sheri one night that he nailed the doors shut so she couldn't enter the house. Sheri said she had thoughts of poisoning Richard because instead of another failed relationship she thought becoming a widow would look better to her friends. Richard became aware of this and began feeding his food first to the dog to see if there was anything wrong with it.

Sheri was searching for something more. She thought there had to be more to this life than what she and Richard were experiencing. She said one day she ran across Pastor Joel and the Lakewood service on TV. Sheri said she wanted to turn the channel, but she just couldn't. Pastor Joel was different from other TV preachers she had seen. He was smiling and talking about a hope she had never heard of and certainly didn't have in her life.

She began watching the program each week and begged Richard to watch with her. She hoped that by watching the program, perhaps Pastor Joel could fix Richard. Even though Richard wouldn't sit and watch the program, he would usually be close by and would listen. Richard thought for sure Sheri was calling Pastor Joel each week and telling him what to say. For some reason, every time Richard would listen in, Pastor Joel would be talking about something Richard was dealing with. He just knew that Sheri must be up to something.

Soon Richard and Sheri began to attend services at Lakewood. They would come in late and sit at the very top of the sanctuary. They didn't want to bother anyone and didn't want anyone bothering them. Sometimes they would come to church after partying all weekend, but even at their lowest point of hopelessness something kept pulling at them to attend. Before long they were attending on a regular basis and were enjoying it. They had heard Pastor Joel say, "Give us a year of your life and come as often as you can. We make you this promise that your life will never be the same!" Richard realized that they had already been attending off and on for a year by then. He leaned over to Sheri and said, "I think we are going to need another year."

Not long after that, they stood at the end of one of the services. They each decided to respond when they heard

Pastor Joel give an invitation for salvation: "If your heart stopped beating in the next few minutes, are you at peace with God? I'm not here to condemn anybody, I just want to help you find a new beginning."

This was what they had been looking for. Richard and Sheri needed a new beginning for their lives and for their marriage. They were excited about this new life in Jesus that they had heard talked about for so long. Jesus was becoming the center of their lives and He was becoming the center of their marriage. Richard and Sheri had finally realized that they couldn't do life successfully without Jesus at the center. This happened more than twelve years ago and because of the new path their lives have been on since they put Jesus at the center, they have a thriving, amazing marriage. They are some of our most devoted marriage teachers at Lakewood Church and have helped many couples. Their motto is, "If Jesus can save us, He can save anyone!"

Because they are both very funny people and God has completely healed them of their past, they have turned their story into a comedy routine. God has opened doors for them to speak at churches, conferences, and retreats, helping other couples meet Jesus and helping wounded marriages to heal through laughter. They sometimes stop and look at their lives in amazement of what God has done. They told us, "We shouldn't have made it."

Keeping Jesus at the center of your marriage sounds like a simple thing and it really can be. It's a step we take daily. Just as Richard and Sheri had to choose to attend church and read the Bible on a regular basis, we also get the opportunity to put Him first place in our hearts daily. Let's be honest, some days we make the right choice and some days we don't. Sometimes it becomes a moment-by-moment choice. Do we trust ourselves at the center or do we put God at the center?

———————

It was obvious to us that we didn't keep Jesus at the center of our marriage during our first five years together. Because we chose not to keep Him at the center, we paid a price and experienced the valley of dry bones. Having a Christ-centered marriage doesn't come with the promise of an easy marriage, but it does come with a promise that through everything we face He will be with us. That's a great promise to remember when you face what seems like insurmountable odds throughout your marriage. It's during those times you can grow closer to God and to each other.

Clayton: We experienced what seemed like an insurmountable challenge a year after we moved to Houston. Do you remember my sackcloth with the *F* for failure? This is more of the story. I was working in the children's ministry full time and Ashlee was a volunteer. She was instrumental in launching many new video and drama elements. During this time Lakewood Church graciously was paying for my health insurance as a full-time employee, and we were paying for Ashlee and our oldest daughter. We were shopping for new health insurance for Ashlee and I decided to cancel their coverage while I looked for something better. Since we had been trying to have another baby for the last two years, I was trying to find insurance that had great maternity coverage. Looking back, canceling the insurance wasn't the best move.

In the spring, I got a call from Ashlee and through her tears I heard her ask me to come home. She was in so much pain that she couldn't get up from the middle of our dining room floor where she had collapsed. I picked up our daughter from daycare and rushed home to find Ashlee still on the floor crying. She had pain in her abdomen that was so severe that she asked me to punch her to put her out of her misery. We quickly took our daughter to a friend's house and I raced Ashlee to the emergency room.

If ever there was a moment we needed Jesus at the center of our lives and our marriage it was that day!

We were finally escorted into the examining room. Ashlee was miserable. After running some tests, they determined she had a cyst the size of a grapefruit and they were scheduling surgery for the next morning. Ashlee had never had surgery and was frightened. I wasn't fearful for her because I knew God was going to watch over her and that she would be fine. But I was fearful for another reason.

I remember kissing Ashlee on the cheek as the pain medicine was finally kicking in so she could sleep. I quietly went out to the parking lot and collapsed in the front seat of our car. An overwhelming feeling of hopelessness filled the car that afternoon. Ashlee had no insurance and it was all my fault! *How much does something like this cost?* I thought. *How is it possible that in the two weeks of her not having insurance this could happen?*

We returned home a few days later. Ashlee was on the road to recovery and we were both thankful that the procedure had been a success. But our joy was soon overshadowed when the next week we were faced with more than forty thousand dollars in doctor and hospital bills.

Immediately I started to think, *How am I going to get us out of this mess?* I was feeling so much pressure and felt it was all on my shoulders. Maybe I should begin looking for a second job or start looking for things to sell around the house. In just a few moments, fear had replaced God at the center of my life. I was going to have to fix this mess I had gotten us into.

For weeks after the surgery, I was still struggling with the weight from this mountain of debt. I didn't want to bring it to Ashlee's attention because she was already depressed—not only because of the debt but because she was told that the cyst was caused by endometriosis. Her hopes of having another child were crushed.

We didn't celebrate the fact that she recovered well from the surgery. We also weren't praising God that as the doctor was removing the cyst he was able to repair the damage that had been caused by the endometriosis. An immense feeling of despondency had overtaken our hope in Jesus and there was no room for anything positive. We were both paralyzed with fear and felt trapped with no way out.

The Mountain of Fear and Debt

We finally came to the point when we couldn't be ruled by this fear anymore. We began to trust God and to speak out against our fears and speak the Word of God over our lives. Jesus said, "If you have faith as a mustard seed, you will say to this mountain, 'Move from here to there,' and it will move; and nothing will be impossible for you" (Matt. 17:20 NKJV).

We had only a small amount of faith, but we started speaking to our mountain. I remember grabbing Ashlee by the hands, getting on our knees, and praying together about the debt. We decided to believe that God would make a way even though we didn't see how. By faith we put God at the center of this situation, and anytime we would start to fear, we would speak the Word of God over our lives. We would speak scriptures like Proverbs 3:5–6: "Lord, we trust in you and we lean not on our own understandings. We acknowledge you and we know that you will make our path straight" or Hebrews 11:6: "You reward those who diligently seek You" (author's paraphrase).

A few weeks later I was in a staff meeting at the church and we were given the opportunity to share prayer requests. Everyone had believed for Ashlee's healing when the surgery happened, but they didn't know she had no insurance or about the massive debt we had incurred. After sharing the details of the story—crying through most of it—someone offered wise counsel. He advised me to wait until all the bills came in and then to contact the hospital and doctors personally. He said to ask, considering we didn't have insurance, what they would take if we could pay them cash in forty-five days or less? I thought, *We don't have any extra cash.* But we decided to speak to that mountain and give it a try.

After a round of phone calls, our forty-thousand-dollar debt was cut down to twenty thousand. This was exciting but still overwhelming. We, however, did not give up hope and decided to speak God's Word to that mountain even louder and with more faith. We used scriptures such as Philippians 4:19, which says, "God will meet all your needs according to the riches of his glory in Christ Jesus." We prayed against fear by speaking 2 Timothy 1:7, "We thank you God that you have not given us a spirit of fear, but of power, love, and a sound mind." "So," we prayed, "we will not walk in fear, we will walk in love, in power, and with a sound mind to hear you clearly."

About a week later we went to the mailbox to find something totally unexpected. It was a sweet letter and a check for ten thousand dollars from a family member who had heard about our situation. We couldn't believe it! We were beyond amazed! We went from forty thousand dollars in debt to twenty thousand dollars and now to ten thousand dollars. But God didn't stop there in answering our prayers.

The next day I received a phone call from a church member who wanted to pay off the rest of our debt. They said, "We want to do this for you. How much should I make the check out for and I will get it in the mail."

I told Ashlee, "You are never going to believe what that phone call was about."

She responded, "Someone offering to pay off the rest of our debt!"

"What?" I said. "How did you know?"

Ashlee said, "After praying and believing God would do it, I just knew it was going to happen! *Mountain be gone!*"

You would think that was the end of the story. God paid off our $40,000! What a miracle that was. But you know it's just like God to show off. Two months later I heard Ashlee screaming from the bathroom. I thought, *Oh no! Not another cyst!* I ran to the bathroom door and shouted, "Are you okay? What's wrong?"

She opened the door with tears in her eyes and held up a positive pregnancy test. "Can you believe it?" she cried.

We wept as we held each other. Two months earlier, we were shedding tears of hopelessness and now we were shedding tears of joy. The mountain had not only moved, it had been destroyed. And we knew without a doubt it was because we put Jesus at the center of our situation.

Praying Together Puts God at the Center

There is so much power that comes from two people praying together, especially a husband and wife. We don't think there could be two greater forces coming against the enemies of life than a husband and wife joining together in prayer. Paul said that the same power that raised Christ from the dead is available to us when we believe in Him (Eph. 1:19–20). Can you imagine the incredible power that you as a couple are activating when you are both believing and standing in agreement through prayer? Praying together is also a way of inviting God into the center of your lives, into every situation. Jesus said, "Again, truly I tell you that if two of you on earth agree about anything they ask for, it will be done for them by my Father in heaven. For where two or three gathers in my name, there am I with them" (Matt. 18:19–20).

Ashlee: Two people that I have witnessed grow in their prayer lives together are my parents. I grew up in a loving home with parents I knew deeply loved and cared for each other. Weekly attendance at church was very important to my mom, so we rarely missed. The importance of getting connected with a church body became ingrained in me, and I will forever be grateful to my parents for that. Even though church was very important, in our house prayer only happened before meals and on special holidays. I didn't ever see my parents pray together while I was growing up, but as an adult I witnessed this become a very important part of their lives.

My parents didn't have much financially when I was kid. Money was always tight. With four kids in the house, our home sometimes seemed too small. My mom loved to cook, but our kitchen was about as big as a medium-sized closet. My parents dreamed of building a big farmhouse on a lot of land with a large kitchen where we could all sit and talk to Mom while she cooked. There were always magazines lying around of house plans and designs my parents loved. They would mark what they loved in those magazines and even began to create their own dream floor plan. They certainly did not have the money at the time to build a house, but that didn't keep them from dreaming, planning, and praying that God would give them the finances to build their dream home one day. I remember seeing these magazines as far back as the 1980s. I often asked, "Are you guys ever going to build this house?"

In 2002, they purchased seven acres of wooded land, but they still didn't have the funds to build the house. Two years later they built a small metal building on the land and began preparing to build. They lived in that small building for five years before they decided it was time to build. My dad told me he walked outside one day and said, "I'm going build that house." And when he said "I," he really meant *him*.

He had taught himself a lot about construction and home remodeling, so he decided he was going to be the head contractor. Later, he realized that he might have taken on too much. That's when my mom said, "We need to start praying together and make sure this is God's plan and His will for us to build."

As they began the building process, they were amazed at how the Lord pulled together even the smallest details. He graced them with people who normally would not have been available, contractors who as a rule only work for builders. They stepped out in faith when our country was in a recession and contractors were hurting for business. From the company building the dirt pad to the painters, they were blessed with many of the top contractors in their area.

Most of the light fixtures and ceiling fans came from a company that was moving locations and had everything on sale for half price.

One company shipped the wrong doors. Since the cost of reordering the doors was more than the company wanted to spend, they offered to give them the doors for free.

For one of their bathrooms, they bought a remnant of a piece of sandstone after they bought a sink, not knowing whether they would go together. When Mom picked up the sink from the store, she opened the box, and her first reaction was, "Oh no, I'm going to have to reorder the sink!" But to her surprise, the sink and sandstone matched perfectly—another one of the times when the Lord orchestrated everything to perfection.

When the granite for the kitchen island was delivered, Mom was so overwhelmed that she exclaimed repeatedly how wonderful it was that God had made this beautiful piece of rock from minerals. She said the workers installing it probably thought she was a bit crazy. She didn't care! She was praising God and giving Him all the glory!

There were so many other God-orchestrated touches in this house, too many to list. My dad said, "I think the most important thing is what we learned from all of this: that it's not about the destination, but it's about the journey, and the journey was about learning to rely on God. It was a lesson in prayer. Your mom and I really prayed together for the first time. That's the blessing, and it continues to this day. Now I know that what we thought we wanted and what God knew we needed were two different things, and we were blessed with this amazing house in the end."

Oh, how our family has enjoyed this house during the last seven years! We have made so many memories and we are grateful for how God has blessed my parents with the miracle of this house.

GOING FURTHER

We want to make sure that you know the hope for your marriage begins and ends with Jesus. When you are placing God in the center of your marriage daily, He can breathe life into dry bones. Speak God's Word over your marriage! Begin praying together each day as a couple. Make this a habit. Start short and sweet and see what happens!

Talking Points

1. Ask your spouse, "Has there ever been a time when a situation we were facing was overwhelming to you?"
2. As a couple, identify some big mountains in your marriage that you need to allow God to deal with.

3. As you begin to pray together as a couple and watch God move on your behalf, what are some things you would like to add to your prayer list?

Epilogue
A Marriage Legacy Worth Leaving

Let this be written for a future generation,
that a people not yet created may praise the LORD.

—PSALM 102:18

The greatest legacy one can pass on to one's
children and grandchildren is not money or
other material things accumulated in one's life,
but rather a legacy of character and faith.

—BILLY GRAHAM

When we were approached about writing a book on marriage, our first response was something like, "Who, us?" We had been married for a little more than twenty years and felt like we had learned a lot, but we didn't have any kind of degree in this area. We love helping couples and sharing with them the mistakes we have made, but we don't consider ourselves marriage experts. Before we married we were quick to offer marriage advice or talk about what we thought a great marriage should be like. Twenty years later we know we will be learning for the rest of our lives how to have a great marriage. We got on our knees and prayed for God's peace and for Him to give us the words as we began writing.

About midway through our writing journey we came across a scripture that set us at ease. "Let this be written for a future generation, that a people not yet created may praise the Lord" (Ps. 102:18).

We realized that our story and the other stories included in *Hope for Your Marriage* are to help this generation and the ones to come. We realized that the hope for our children's marriages begins at home, when they are still young. We don't want our children to make the same mistakes that we made. "By wisdom a house is built, and through understanding it is established; through knowledge its rooms are filled with rare and beautiful treasures" (Prov. 24:3–4).

We want our house to be built on wisdom and we need to pass that wisdom on to our children, so they can pass it on to their children and so on. What a tragedy it would be for God to work a miracle in someone's life that he or she didn't share with others.

This is our story of what God has done for us and for many others. This is our testimony of God's faithfulness in our marriage, and oh, how we have prayed for you who are reading this book right now, that something we have written will help you in some way.

Your Story Matters

We want to assure you that your story matters as well. Someone needs to hear your story. People need to be encouraged by what God has done in you and in your marriage. You may feel as though you haven't got it all figured out yet and that is perfect! Just be willing to share your story with your children, your friends, and even with strangers as opportunities present.

We can assure you that *there is hope for your marriage.* As you are willing to do whatever it takes to have the marriage you have always dreamed of, God will begin to work in you and through you to do His great pleasure. He will open doors and set up divine appointments so that you can tell your story and give God all the credit. One of our favorite scriptures is 2 Corinthians 12:9: "My grace is sufficient for you, for my power is made perfect in weakness." The Lord loves using weak people because He then gets all the credit and others see what He can do and how much He loves us.

Words for a Couple About to Be Married

From Clayton to the Groom

Hello, just wanted to take a few minutes to encourage you. You and I probably don't know each other and it might not have been your choice to read this book. If you will indulge me for a few minutes, I want to help you prepare for your marriage in the hopes that you and your bride will enjoy an amazing, fulfilling, lifelong relationship! These are some of the things I wish someone had told me before I got married.

After you marry, you might have an overwhelming urge to fix every problem that presents itself. If you want to fix things around your house or your apartment, that's great. But remember that your wife may not want you to be her personal Mr. Fix It. This was a problem for me early on, and, honestly, I still struggle with this.

When Ashlee told me about troubles she was having on her job or in other areas of her life, I assumed she wanted me to come to her rescue. But she didn't want my help. Your wife may be different, but if I had to make a wager, I would bet she is a lot like my wife. A few years into our marriage, Ashlee told me, "Please quit trying to fix my problems and just listen to me!"

(We discussed this in length earlier in the book. Ashlee explained how she felt I must think she was inadequate when I kept trying to fix everything for her.)

I promptly replied, "Well, quit telling me all your problems!"

I admit that wasn't the smartest thing to say. My advice is that when your wife comes to you with her problems, just simply respond, "Honey, I'm so sorry you are facing this. I just want you to know that I am here for you and I'm ready to listen. Together, we can get through this!" Your wife needs to be reminded that you are by her side.

The next thing may seem a little far out there but please trust me on this one. Whatever you did to win your bride, make sure you *continue* to do those things after you marry. Continue calling or texting her and asking her out for date nights. Open doors for her and pull out her chair. Without saying a word, you are telling her that she is cherished and valuable. (Remember how we stopped having long conversations after we were married and how disappointed Ashlee was?)

Whatever you do, don't ever let anything come between you and your daily time with God. Each day set time aside to pray for your wife. Allow God to speak to you through His word. Remember you have a job to do: "Husbands, love your wives, just as Christ loved the church and gave himself up for her" (Eph. 5:25). We are called to love our wives sacrificially just as Jesus loved the church. That simply looks like a husband who is willing to lay down his pride, his rights, and his will for his wife. When husbands do this, it's easy for wives to do their part, which is also mentioned in Ephesians 5. It's our job as husbands to set the standard by submitting to God and His will for our lives.

From Ashlee to the Bride

I remember being so stressed out in the days leading up to our wedding. I wanted everything to be perfect. This seems to be true for all the brides-to-be we counsel. There is always so much to be done before the big day and sometimes there is added family drama that makes it even more challenging. (Remember our discussion about fairy-tale weddings?) One of the sweetest and most beautiful weddings I ever attended was my sister Lauren's. My brother and I got married at very young ages, but it took my sister a little longer to find her beloved.

Lauren and Louis: March 13, 2015, at the age of thirty-one, Lauren said, "I do," and what a precious ceremony it was. She and Louis were married outdoors in a very beautiful place in East Texas, surrounded by big trees and pasture areas. That day, however, had all the makings of a disaster. The forecast that morning was heavy rain and cold temperatures. I was stressed for her, continually asking my mom what was plan B. There wasn't a strong plan B, but my sister never seemed worried. She told me later that she was confident in what God would do that day and it brought her peace.

It rained a lot that morning but cleared up about an hour before the wedding. We were grateful, but it was still cold and there were mud puddles where she would be standing during the ceremony. She wore a simple, but beautiful, white lace dress with a train. And as she walked toward Louis her train started getting muddy, but she didn't care and he didn't either. Their eyes were locked on each other and tears were streaming down Louis's face.

They had decided that during the ceremony they would wash each other's feet to represent what Jesus did for His disciples. It was also their way of demonstrating how they would humble themselves in marriage. Lauren's turn to have her feet washed came first, and when I saw the mud puddle Louis was kneeling in to wash her feet, I stood by my sister as her matron of honor and thought, *Oh no! She can't do this. No! Don't do this, Lauren. Your dress will be ruined!* Where she would be kneeling was right beside the groomsmen, so I thought, *Okay, they will pick up her train when she starts to kneel. Surely, they will do that.* Well, do you think they did that? Of course not.

I kept trying to get their attention with facial expressions. If looks could kill, every one of those groomsmen would be dead. Not one of them helped her. As she knelt to wash Louis's feet, her train was drenched in a sea of mud. I was mortified for her and desperately tried to figure out what to do. Lauren, however, could not have cared less. All she cared about was marrying Louis and her focus was all on him. I couldn't concentrate on the rest of the ceremony; all I could do was look at her dress and think about how disappointed Lauren would be when she saw how muddy it was.

After the ceremony, Clayton walked up to me, his face red from crying. I asked if he was okay. He said, "Ashlee, that was one of the most beautiful wedding ceremonies I have ever seen."

"*What?!* But didn't you see all the mud on her dress?" I asked.

"Yeah," he said. "But I was so focused on the ceremony that I didn't really think about it. Everyone around me was crying because of the sacrificial innocence and vulnerability they were exposing to everyone. You could definitely sense the presence of God over them."

"Really?" I said. "I was so focused on her dress and the mud and wanting to knock the groomsmen over the head with my bouquet that I missed it."

I missed it.

I was so caught up in what I thought was a disaster that I missed what God was doing. Bride, I say this to you: let those details go. Just enjoy the moment, enjoy the day, and go on to enjoy your lives together. Don't get caught up in things not always going the way you planned. Don't let the disappointments of life blur your eyes and heart to what God is trying to do in your marriage and in your life. My sister danced and laughed the entire evening. She did not care about her muddy dress. She only cared about enjoying the moment she had been waiting for since she was a little girl and about making precious memories with Louis and her friends and family.

I would also say to a new bride, honor your husband in everything. Honor him even when he doesn't deserve it. Sometimes the only way to do that is with God's help. Spend time in prayer every day asking God to help you honor your husband in everything. Don't speak poorly of your husband, especially to your mom. Your mom is probably your mother bear and will always want to protect her little cub, but complaining to her about your husband has the potential to lead to heartache and hurt your marriage.

Your husband is most likely a Mr. Fix It man. If you tell him about something you are going through, he is most likely going to want to fix it. But you might want him to just listen. Tell him that. Men don't know that sometimes we just like to share what we're facing and only want a hug and for you to tell us it's going to be okay. Even to this day, before I tell Clayton about something I am going through, I let him know if I want him to just listen or if I want him to fix it. He loves that!

Words for Someone Who Has Been Married for a While

We would love to encourage you to tell your story. There are many couples who could gain from your experience. Invest in the next generation by helping them find hope for their marriages. Many younger couples are looking for people who are further along on the marriage journey. They can learn from your triumphs and your tragedies. Your story doesn't have to be perfect; it just needs to be authentic. We meet couples at different stages of their marriages who are looking for mentors.

You may feel the same as we did early on in our marriage. Maybe you aren't sure how you got there, but now that you have been married for a few years, you find yourselves in the bottom of a valley of dry bones. We can tell you that you aren't alone and there is hope for your marriage! Don't give up! Begin to declare hope just as Ezekiel did over those dry bones.

Talk with your spouse and invite him or her out on a date and begin to pursue each other again. Find a good marriage counselor or a pastor and talk through some of the issues that you are facing. Pray with your spouse each day. Your prayer time doesn't have to be long and drawn out but needs to be heartfelt.

Decide to do one thing today that will breathe life back into your marriage. After you do that, get ready to do something else tomorrow, and the next day, and so on until you begin to see your marriage transforming.

Hope is available for all marriages. Begin small but stay consistent. Before long you will be writing your own book to help others!

It's Never Too Late

Clayton: When Ashlee and I began dating, we each had great expectations of what we wanted in a spouse. We both agreed on the importance of family. Our families had played a huge role in developing our views and character. She has an amazing mother and father who have taught her what love and commitment is all about. They set the bar high.

We have learned so much from them over the years. They model the importance of keeping God at the center of each of their hearts and at the center of their marriage. They make it a priority to pray together every day regardless of how busy they are. They didn't start out that way, but they have taken courageous steps over the years to get to a healthy place in their marriage.

Growing up, family was everything to me. God always played a vital role in our family. My parents met during high school, playing Mary and Joseph in a live nativity at their local church. Jesus was in the center of that nativity scene then and He still is at the center of their relationship more than fifty years later. Looking back over the years, I remember always being involved in church and watching my parents read their Bibles regularly.

My parents have always had a good marriage—not a perfect marriage, but definitely good. I think back to that time when they were courageous enough to both identify areas they needed to work on in their relationship and I admire them so much for doing that. Throughout the years they have continued to listen to teaching tapes, read books, and attend conferences to grow in their marriage. You would think after fifty-plus years of marriage they would be coasting into their golden years.

On their fifty-fifth wedding anniversary, instead of going on a once in a lifetime trip to celebrate, they wanted to attend our Spark marriage conference at Lakewood Church. We told them it was okay, they didn't have to come just to support us. And they told us, "We realize that but we are coming to grow in our marriage. Once we stop learning, we stop growing." We got to honor them that evening of the event in front of thousands of people. It was a night I will never forget."

My dad took another courageous step a few years ago. Before I tell you what that step was, let me tell you a little about Dad. I was like most boys who wanted to be like their fathers. There was no one I wanted to hang out with more than my dad. When I was three years old I would go into his room and get one of his T-shirts to wear to bed. We would often take his old, white VW bug and drive to the local donut shop on Saturday mornings.

My dad has been my hero for as long as I can remember, but he wasn't perfect. He grew up as an only child with parents who loved him but showed their affection in different ways. For example, it was normal for his dad not to hug him. His dad showed love and affection by working hard to provide for their family, so it was "normal" for my dad to show his love and affection in the same way. (Remember discussing the different "normals" we all grew up with?)

My dad was a banker and worked diligently to provide for our family. My dad didn't always want to throw the ball around with me outside, but he made sure that I was well taken care of and that I was brought up in a loving home committed to God and a strong work ethic. He would tell me that he loved me but it was only after I told him, and it was always a little awkward for him.

As I have grown older and become a dad myself, there is still no one I look up to more than my father. My father has quietly and constantly shown me how to be a man of integrity and a man after God's own heart. The story I am about to share with you is something that has solidified my father's hero status for life. It may not seem like much to you, but it was the most impactful thing my dad ever did for me. At the age of seventy-two, my dad took the time to write my brother, sister, and me each a letter. He personalized them and I'm not sure what he told the others, but what he shared with me shook me to my core.

When I first received the letter, I didn't think that much about it. Since it had my parent's address and looked so formal, I knew immediately it must be from my dad. As I mentioned before, my dad was a banker and a very organized man. I thought maybe he was sending information on their next trip as he always does, complete with an agenda of daily activities and phone numbers listed in case of an emergency.

As I began to read, I quickly realized that this was no such agenda. This was a personal letter to me from my dad, something I had never received before. Tears began to fill my eyes as I started reading this letter written with honesty and love. Here is a small portion of what was written.

Dear Clayton,

Recently, the Lord has impressed on me the need to write each of you children a letter about how proud I am and how much I love you. Clayton, you are an outstanding husband, father, and pastor. Your influence on the lives of so many will not be known here on earth. God has given you a great responsibility as well as opportunity. It makes me feel so proud of you to see all you are doing.

I have loved you from that first day they put you in my arms at Good Shepherd Hospital back in 1971. I felt so lucky to have another son in our family. And I will always remember your wedding because Ashlee is exactly who you needed and I am so happy to call her my daughter-in-law.

Needless to say, we all have made our share of mistakes, but that is the way we have to learn many lessons in life. I know you remember the sermon we both heard about being a diamond and how God is always trimming off the rough edges. Sometimes it seems that we have to go through some of the same situations over and over before God finally gets our attention. I guess we all grow up just doing things like our parents. My dad never really expressed his pride or love for me, although I think he loved me. That was my example, but I thought it was time I corrected that. Of all the things I have in my life, I am most proud of all my children.

I love you,

Dad

By the time I finished this letter I was doing the ugly cry. I was so grateful that my dad was willing to take a courageous step and send me this letter. He taught me something valuable. I knew that he loved me and he was proud of me, but he finally told me. You might be thinking, *But it was in a letter?* For me, however, it meant more that he would take the time to sit down, write a letter, buy a stamp, and mail it to me, than if he had just picked up the phone. He also showed me that regardless of how long you have been doing something a specific way, you can always take a step outside of your "normal" and have a lasting impact on someone you love!

In the top drawer of my desk at the church, I have a place I keep things that serve as "memorial stones." Things that may not have any value to others but are priceless to me. My father's letter along with its envelope are in that drawer. Every time I see that letter in my drawer, it reminds me that my father loves me and is proud of me. The letter also reminds me that I want to be like my dad and never be afraid to take courageous steps to make a change, regardless of how old I am.

Your Legacy Starts Now

A simple definition of legacy is "something that is passed down from one generation to the next." It can be something good that is passed down for multiple generations or it could be something negative that a younger generation determines not to continue. Regardless of what the marriage legacy has been for you and your family, the good news is that a new legacy can start now.

Maybe the "normal" marriage or family you had growing up wasn't the best model and you believed you were destined to pass this down to your children. We want to encourage you that a new legacy can begin at any time. Taking even simple steps, before long you can have changed the culture of your marriage and have a new legacy to pass down to future generations.

Ashlee: When we made the decision to humble ourselves and work on our marriage at year five, it wasn't always easy. There were days when one of us was unkind or selfish, but we had to choose agapē love regardless. We had to take steps toward restoration whether or not our spouse took steps that day. We spent each morning in prayer, asking God to give us the ability to love like He loves.

I prayed this scripture over us consistently: "Satisfy us in the morning with your unfailing love, that we may sing for joy and be glad all our days" (Ps. 90:14). During a time when Clayton wasn't satisfying me, God was filling that gap until we got to a place of restoration and of great joy.

Now, regardless of what I go through each day, Clayton, my beloved, has my back and is always on my side. I can't imagine going through life without him. He is my best friend, my lover, my confidant, and my biggest cheerleader. But he would have never become these things to me if I had not chosen to love him. We would *never* be where we are today based on feelings. We had to choose to love. Even on days when we did not feel like it.

I am so grateful that God helped us get out of that valley of dry bones. I think of what our marriage would be like now (or if it even would have survived) if we had not taken those steps toward our promised land and I want to fall to my knees in thankfulness to God. He is our *only hope* for marriage. He is our *only hope* to get out of that valley. He is our *only hope* for complete restoration. He is our *only hope* to get to our promised land. He is our *only hope* for leaving a legacy of a strong marriage for the next generation.

Will you make the decision today to do whatever it takes to have the marriage you have always hoped and dreamed of? Hope for your marriage begins with a decision to take a single step that will lead you out of your valley of dry bones and into your promised land. "Fight for your families, your sons and your daughters, your wives and your homes" (Neh. 4:14).

God is for your family, God is for your marriage. Fight for them. Fight with the sword of the Spirit and the shield of faith. We know you can do it. If God could do it for us, for Richard and Sheri, for Mike and Jennifer, for Jason and Staci, for Craig and Samantha, for Miguel and Laura, and for Joel and Shawna, He can do it for you. Will you take that step? God is graciously waiting for you.

GOING FURTHER

A legacy is something that is passed down from one generation to another. We can pass down a hope-filled legacy of marriage to our children and to others who are yet to be married. It's important to begin by sharing your challenges and your successes with others. Continue your legacy today by pouring into the next generation and give them the hope they need for an amazing marriage.

Talking Points

1. Share five things with your spouse that you have learned about marriage from previous generations.
2. During the next two weeks, find a couple who have been married a shorter time than you have and spend some time with them. Let them ask you anything they want about your marriage. Be willing to share your challenges and successes.
3. Do you know a couple this book might help? If so, consider gifting a copy of this book and pray over it before you give it to them.

Acknowledgments

From beginning to the very end, we give Jesus all the credit for this book. We never went looking for this opportunity, but God's plans for us are so much bigger than we could have ever imagined. He continues to open so many amazing doors as we keep Him at the center of our lives and marriage.

To our parents, Bill, Judy, Tim, and Melissa. We can't thank you enough for building a legacy of marriage in us by loving each other. We are incredibly grateful for all the sacrifices you have made for us. If this book helps any marriage, know that you played a huge part in that.

To our children, Addison, Aubree, and Colton. You are our greatest treasures and we love each of you so much. Thank you for being so understanding during this process. You are our favorites!

We want to thank our amazing pastors Joel and Victoria for your leadership and support of this book from the beginning. Thank you to Dr. Paul, Jennifer, Kevin, Lisa, and Ms. Dodie for your commitment to loving God and loving people.

Pastor Craig and Samantha, thank you for your friendship and encouragement. You are some of our biggest cheerleaders and we love doing life with you both.

Brittany, you are a true blessing and a God-send for us. Thank you for always having our backs.

To the entire staff of Lakewood Church, and all our amazing marriage teachers and volunteers, thank you! We are truly honored to serve alongside some of the greatest people in the world!

To Debby Jackson. Thank you for being obedient to God and giving us the encouragement we needed to write this book. We will be forever grateful for you.

To all our Thomas Nelson and Emanate family, thank you for loving us and walking with us through this process. Joel Kneedler, you started this all and we are grateful to God for you. To Janene MacIvor, Joey Paul, and Cody Van Ryn, thank you for your incredible God-given gifts. You inspire us!

Notes

1. Henry George Liddell, Robert Scott, *A Greek-English Lexicon*.
2. R. E. O. White, *Baker Encyclopedia of the Bible*, vol. 2 (Grand Rapids, MI: Baker Book House, 1988), 1357.
3. Lily Koppel, *The Astronaut Wives Club: A True Story* (NY: Red Leather Diary, 2013).
4. Charlie and Dotty Duke, *MoonWalker* (Nashville: Thomas Nelson, 1990), 100.
5. Ibid., 244.
6. Ibid., 261.
7. Achtemeier, P. J., Harper & Row and Society of Biblical Literature (1985). In *Harper's Bible Dictionary* (1st ed., p. 890) San Francisco: Harper & Row.

About the Authors

PHOTOGRAPHY BY MATTHEW DANIEL

Clayton and Ashlee Hurst are the marriage and parenting pastors at Lakewood Church in Houston, Texas. Married for more than twenty years, Clayton and Ashlee share a passion to see God breathe life into every couple they encounter, strengthening and enriching their family. Clayton and Ashlee also serve as the hosts of Lakewood's annual Spark Marriage Conference, featuring well-known marriage experts and with an attendance of more than eight thousand people from around the world. They are the parents of three children and live in the Houston area.